THE DUCHESS OF
DEVONSHIRE'S BALL

SOPHIA MURPHY

THE DUCHESS OF DEVONSHIRE'S BALL

Foreword by
THE DUCHESS OF DEVONSHIRE

*

SIDGWICK & JACKSON
London

To Joyce and Liz, with love

First published in Great Britain in 1984
by Sidgwick & Jackson Limited

Copyright © 1984 Sophia Murphy

I S B N 0-283-98988-2

Designed by James Campus

Printed in Great Britain by
Biddles Ltd., Guildford, Surrey

for Sidgwick & Jackson Limited
1 Tavistock Chambers, Bloomsbury Way
London W C 1 A 2 S G

ACKNOWLEDGEMENTS

I would like to express my warmest thanks to all those who helped me with my book, especially Anita Leslie, who took such trouble on my behalf; Peter Day, Keeper of the Collection, and Michael Pearman, Librarian at Chatsworth, who both helped with research; Alastair Forsyth, Ian Leith and Margaret Reeder at the National Monuments Record; Amanda Herries at the Museum of London; and Deborah Moore at the *Illustrated London News*.

I am also indebted to my mother and father for all their help and support, to Nick Ashley for his penetrating historical insights, to Clarissa Baring for her moral support and sense of humour, and to Margaret Willes, my editor.

The majority of the illustrations reproduced in the book are taken from an album presented to the Duchess of Devonshire in 1897. It was compiled by the principal guests at the Devonshire House Ball, and contained their portraits in the costumes that they wore that evening. I am most grateful to my parents for allowing me to reproduce these photographs. I should also like to thank the following for providing illustrations and granting permission for their use: Trustees of Chatsworth Settlement, 22, 28, 31, 35, 37, 40/41g, 49, 73, 161b, 164a and b, 170; *Country Life*, 40/1a, b, c, d, e, f, 161a; Greater London Council, 38; *Illustrated London News*, 13, 139; By permission of the governors of Kimbolton School: photograph: Courtauld Institute of Art, 23; Museum of London, 35a and b; National Portrait Gallery, 46, 58; Radio Times Hulton Picture Library, 25, 123; Royal Commission of Historical Monuments (England), 169; Trustees of the Tate Gallery, 57b.

FOREWORD
BY THE DUCHESS OF DEVONSHIRE

A fancy dress ball only lasts a few hours. Compared to other reasons for dressing up, like acting in plays, ballets and operas which can be repeated night after night, a ball is as ephemeral as a dream. Yet, once having accepted the invitation, serious grown-up people will take endless trouble and go to extraordinary lengths, and often suffer extreme discomfort, to appear on the one and only night as their chosen character.

The enthusiasm is infectious and the grumbling about what a bother it all is is forgotten in the spirit of competition which goads on the *invitées* to make sure their clothes are more beautiful, authentic, outrageous or funny than their neighbours'.

The Devonshire House fancy dress ball has become a legend. Until Sophy began to find out more about it I thought that, like many legends, over the years it had become exaggerated to a ridiculous degree. I was wrong.

In the days when a ball was given on four or five nights a week in May, June and July, when the now vanished private houses of London were going full blast, it had to be a very special entertainment to arouse much interest. The Duchess of Devonshire's ball was a very special entertainment.

It was not difficult for her to mobilize the female guests. The women who were invited had little to do but arrange themselves for such an occasion and one can easily picture the excitement and pleasure it gave them to do so. Most of their dresses were wonderfully imaginative and worth all the time and trouble spent over them. But even the clever old Duchess must have surprised herself by persuading a lot of middle-aged

[7]

men to take the trouble to order their costumes and to suffer the tedium of trying them on.

That she was able to persuade her husband to give the party in the first place shows how indulgent he was towards her. The Duke was sixty-four in 1897. He was responsible for education and defence in the coalition government of Lloyd George and Lord Salisbury. No one could describe him as a frivolous man and his idea of a pleasurable evening was a game of bridge with his wife and some old friends. One can only imagine how he must have groaned and sighed at the prospect of the night's entertainment on the 2 July; but he entered into the spirit of the thing to please his adored wife.

Perhaps Englishmen secretly love dressing up. Perhaps by pretending to be somebody else they lose the self-consciousness with which so many of them are plagued.

Certainly at any ceremonial occasion, whether military, ecclesiastic, academic, in the City of London or at Westminster, it is the men who wear fancy dress, appearing in cocks' feathers and sables, ermine and swords, even carrying posies of flowers through the streets, while their women melt into the surroundings like hen pheasants in the bracken.

Luckily for the readers of this book the guests all submitted themselves to the boredom of being photographed for the privately printed album presented to the Duchess of Devonshire by her friends. Many of these remarkable pictures are reproduced here. The expressionless faces of the subjects remind us of the long exposures necessary for photography ninety years ago.

Fashion has changed as to what is considered beautiful and, looking at the photographs of the women (with a few glittering exceptions like the Duchesses of Portland and Marlborough), one finds it hard to imagine the sitters as the heart-breakers they certainly were. One could be forgiven for questioning if they possessed hearts, or any other organs for that matter, as they seem to be made of wood or some harder material, standing set as concrete, against the photographer's backcloths.

Fifty-four years passed before a fancy dress ball comparable to the Devonshire House Ball was given. In many ways it was like the subject of this book. Discussed for months beforehand, it created desperate jealousy between the people who were asked and the people who were not. There were *entrées* arranged by professional designers as determined to outdo one another as the arrangers of the parades at Devonshire House.

The difference was that the guests arrived in gondolas instead of carriages because the ball was given in Venice to celebrate the rebirth of the Palazzo Labia. The munificent host was Charles de Beistegui and the year was 1951. Andrew and I were lucky enough to be invited.

Several impressions have lasted in my mind. One was the entrance of Jacques Fath, a well-known Paris dressmaker at that time, wearing a headdress of ostrich feathers as tall as himself and shimmering in a gold lamé jacket and a sort of golden skirt slashed with white satin. Another was Daisy Fellowes, famed for her elegance and regularly voted the Best Dressed Woman by Americans, who went as The Americas from the Tiepolo painting on the staircase wall of the residence of the Prince Bishop at Würzburg in Germany. There was a decidedly Red Indian flavour in this *entrée* and her attendants were stained brown. Her dress was a vast affair of billowing chiffon printed in a pattern of leopard skin, the first time this was seen. Afterwards it became high fashion and everything from luggage to furnishing material appeared in leopard skin design.

The Tiepolo fresco on the walls of the Palazzo Labia portrays Antony and Cleopatra. So many women threatened to be Cleopatra that the host, seeing trouble ahead, thought it best to decide the matter himself and nominated Diana Cooper for the role.

Another similarity to the subject of this book was that a friend of mine, who described to me how much she enjoyed watching it all without having to take part, arrived at the back door and climbed to the gallery of the great reception room where she saw the assembly of the *entrées* and all that was happening, unencumbered by fancy dress. She was not in mourning, like poor Mrs Hwfa Williams. She just could not be bothered to dress up.

Charles de Beistegui went one better than the Devonshires. He provided wine and food and entertainment on the *campo* outside for the citizens of Venice, and at least one Frenchman of noble birth, who thought he should have been asked to the ball, enjoyed himself immensely among the crowd who were climbing greasy poles for chickens and hams.

[9]

He was visited every now and again by the glamorous figures who came out from the palazzo.

In the 1930s my sisters used to go to the Chelsea Arts Ball at the Royal Albert Hall on New Year's Eve. They came back with thrilling tales of the wild behaviour and daring costumes of the participants.

The best fancy dress I have ever seen was at the Carnival in Rio de Janeiro in the early fifties. A South American international polo team dressed as English governesses arrived at a smart restaurant, which was full of people in extravagantly theatrical get-ups. The 'governesses' wore quiet navy blue crêpe de chine dresses with white collars, straw hats put straight on their heads, jade earrings and strings of beads, black lace gloves and square white handbags hanging on their hairy arms. There was nothing so simple or so funny at Devonshire House.

In spite of the rooms full of papers at Chatsworth there is surprisingly little to tell us about Devonshire House and practically nothing about the ball. Sophy set herself the task of finding out about it from contemporary letters and memoirs, and such was the fame of the ball that it became more a question of what to leave out than what to put in.

Devonshire House was sold by the 9th Duke of Devonshire in 1919. In 1924 its new owners pulled it down. The furniture remains, and even the silk off the walls, spread about Chatsworth. Some of the doors and chimney pieces were used at Birch Grove, Harold Macmillan's house in Sussex. The billiard room doors have removable panels to let the smoke out. Other chimney pieces lie on their backs in the forge by the stables at Chatsworth and in the granary loft above are stored gilded fillets, extravagantly carved and painted pelmets, the London state harness of the carriage horses and other grubby and tattered remains of its old glory. In the kitchen maids' bedrooms silk curtains, cushions, tassels and braids are piled high.

Just before the house was sold someone took a photograph of Billy Hartington, my brother-in-law. He was two years old, and stood on the wide and shallow steps at the curve of the staircase leading to the saloon and other reception rooms which had been the highly decorated background for people and parties since William Kent rebuilt it after a fire in 1733. The photograph is doubly sad. Billy was killed in action in 1944.

Twenty years earlier the house disappeared in a pile of dust and rubble. The destruction of the house is one of many such tragedies of the last sixty years. It is not much comfort to think it would not be allowed to be pulled down now. It has gone for ever and with it the elegance of the ghosts of 1897 whose everyday clothes are fancy dress now.

*The Diamond Jubilee of the Queen-Empress, 1897. This is the 'Illustrated London
News' tribute to the aged Queen, showing subjects from all parts of her Empire
acknowledging not only Victoria, but the Prince of Wales and the Duke of York
standing behind her throne, and her great-grandson, the little Prince Edward,
sitting at her feet. This was to demonstrate the strength of the succession, for they
were to become in turn Edward VII, George V and Edward VIII. In the
background the artist has depicted St Paul's Cathedral where a thanksgiving
service was held for the Queen on 22 June*

[12]

THE year 1897 was to prove a glorious one in British history : it was the year of Victoria's Diamond Jubilee. Subjects flooded in from all over the world to pay homage to their Queen and Empress. During the weeks of celebrations, London was bursting with potentates and emissaries, rajahs and princes from all over the Empire, as well as contingents from every imperial army and police force.

The people of Britain were inflamed with excitement. Society hostesses entertained with more gusto than ever, and many, like the Duchess of Devonshire, used the Jubilee as an excuse for lavish parties. In the countryside villages were hung with miles of red, white and blue bunting, bonfires were built on hill tops ready for Jubilee Night on 22 June, and squires gave Jubilee dinners for their workers and tenants. Rich and poor alike were united in their enthusiasm for Queen, Country and Empire.

For the Diamond Jubilee gave Britain the opportunity not only to celebrate sixty years of the much-loved Queen's rule, but also to demonstrate the magnitude of her Empire and imperial achievements. By 1897 Queen Victoria ruled over nearly a quarter of the world's land and nearly a quarter of its population. Her territories were widely scattered across the globe, governed by thousands of officials whose job it was to undertake, in Kipling's words, 'the white man's burden'. The seas surrounding them were protected by the legendary British Navy.

During the 1880s, fear of competition from other countries in acquiring colonies, and the likelihood of their imposing trade tariffs, provoked Britain into securing huge areas of tropical and sub-tropical territory. In Africa, Cecil Rhodes was preparing the way for the creation of further dominions to be developed jointly by the British and the Dutch under the protection of the Crown.

Throughout the 1890s enthusiasm for the Empire gained momentum. The concept of New Imperialism fired the imagination of the English people, and was embraced with fervour by all classes. Jingoism was whipped up by the popular press and became the favourite theme of music-halls, while sayings such as 'an Empire upon which the sun never sets' were in common use.

The emphasis placed on imperialism by the Conservative and Liberal Unionist Alliance helped enormously towards their victory in the election of 1895. In this Government led by Lord Salisbury, Joseph Chamberlain took office as Colonial Secretary, and quickly set to work to improve the administration and unity of the Empire. He introduced a penny post throughout the colonies under British suzerainty, and provided loans for undeveloped lands and other enterprises. Above all, he convinced colonial administrators of the Government's sympathy and desire to co-operate.

By 1897 the Empire seemed secure and invincible. Gladstone, with his anti-imperialist views, had resigned in 1894, and even Ireland, a constant fly in the ointment with her frequent outbursts of dissatisfaction over British rule, had simmered down to a sullen silence.

The wealth of jingoism and patriotism that had been boiling up throughout the 1890s found an outlet in the Diamond Jubilee. The procession which took place on 22 June was the culmination of the patriotic fervour that inspired the nation in that summer of 1897. The Queen, accompanied by 50,000 troops, was driven through the streets of London for the thanksgiving service outside St Paul's Cathedral, where she was greeted by her family, headed by the Prince and Princess of Wales. The crowds turned out in their thousands. Every window overlooking the six-mile route, every inch of space available on the streets, was filled with cheering, flag-waving subjects, the majority of whom had never known another sovereign.

But, despite the euphoria of that summer and the apparent invincibility of Britain's power as a nation, there were rumbling indications that her supremacy was under threat. France and Germany had extended their colonies and were building new navies; both were bitterly jealous and resentful of England's power, as was demonstrated by their hostile reaction in 1895 to the Jameson Raid in South Africa. In the United States and Germany technical and industrial advances were progressing in leaps and bounds, but their products were protected by tariffs imposed on imported goods. Meanwhile Britain, despite these threats to her industrial power, held on stubbornly to her policy of Free Trade.

By 1897 Britain's Golden Age of agriculture, which had flourished during the 1860s and 1870s, was long since over. In 1879 came the first in a series of bad harvests, and the failing of crops in England coincided with the importation of cheap food from abroad. Acres of virgin soil in America were reaped and huge quantities of grain were transported to the coast by the rapidly expanding railways, there to be shipped across the Atlantic.

During the 1880s and 1890s, quicker ocean crossings and the innovation of refrigeration on ships resulted in a glut of meat from North and South America and Australia. Farmers in Britain lost capital and had to reduce rents, and unemployment amongst agricultural labourers was rife, resulting in thousands flooding to the already overcrowded cities in search of work.

The agricultural slump and the challenge from abroad affected all landowners, and those of the aristocracy who relied solely on their land for income were forced to lower their standard of living. Many, however, had additional sources of income such as coal and other mines, or large chunks of valuable property in the larger cities. Others, feeling the bite of the depression, increased their investments in stocks and shares and took directorships of companies to supplement their incomes.

Despite this, the majority of the aristocracy was living more extravagantly than ever. The big estates were run along almost feudal lines, with large quantities of servants employed to look after the huge houses and their inhabitants, while hostesses, encouraged by the Prince of Wales, vied with each other to provide lavish entertainments.

The composition of what was known as 'society' was altering as the century was drawing to its close. Earlier strict boundaries were now much less rigidly defined. A large number of peerages had been granted to those who had made fortunes from industry : bankers and brewers were able to gain entry not only to society drawing rooms but to both Houses of

Parliament. Men like Henry Asquith – a barrister – and Joseph Chamberlain – a Birmingham businessman – mixed freely with old Establishment figures such as the Duke of Devonshire and the Marquis of Salisbury.

Despite this tendency, the aristocracy and landed gentry continued to hold the upper hand in political leadership, and until Campbell Bannerman's Government of 1906 they still supplied the majority in every Cabinet. Beneath the surface, however, there were movements and changes taking place that would slowly undermine the foundations of the old order. In 1885 the Fabian Society was founded by George Bernard Shaw and Sidney Webb, two middle-class intellectuals who had concluded that since the phlegmatic British could not be roused to overthrow capitalism by revolution, the solution was to take over the capitalist system by a process of steady infiltration. In Scotland, and later in England, Keir Hardie was working strenuously for Socialism and the unemployed, while all over the country labour forces, much facilitated by the progress in communications, were beginning to organize themselves.

In 1894, the year in which death duties were introduced, the Independent Labour Party was founded, and although in the election of 1895 each of the twenty-seven candidates put up was defeated, the Labour movement throughout the country was quickly gaining momentum.

Only the better informed of the aristocracy were aware of the tremors beneath the surface. To most of them, supremely confident in their position of wealth and power, the idea of change in the social order was inconceivable. And few enjoyed greater wealth and power than the 8th Duke and his wife, who chose in that hot summer of celebrations to throw the most magnificent entertainment of the century: the Devonshire House Ball.

SPENCER Compton Cavendish, 8th Duke of Devonshire, was born on 23 July 1833, the eldest son of the 2nd Earl of Burlington of the second creation. The earldom had become extinct on the death of the 3rd Earl in 1753, but was recreated in 1831 for William Cavendish, Spencer Compton's grandfather.

When he was born, it did not seem likely that Spencer Compton would inherit the Devonshire title, as the 6th Duke was forty-three years old and it was presumed that sooner or later he would marry and produce an heir. This was not to be. In 1858 the 6th Duke died unmarried, and Spencer Compton's father, a grandson of the 6th Duke's uncle and thus a fairly distant relation, inherited the dukedom, and Spencer Compton took the courtesy title of Marquis of Hartington.

Spencer Compton's mother had died when he was seven, a blow from which his father never recovered (it is said that he never smiled again). However, he was a kind and dutiful father to his daughter and three sons and, having loathed the harsh regime of Eton, he kept his sons at home where he tutored them himself.

The four children led a sheltered life at Holker Hall, their beautiful house in the Lake District. They rarely left home, spending their days, when not at lessons, riding and fishing on the estate. So it is not surprising that when, in 1851, Spencer Compton went up to Trinity College, Cambridge, he was quite unprepared for the kind of life that he found there. The other undergraduates of his social standing seemed interested only in gambling, drinking and fast living in general; scholarship and

Spencer Compton Cavendish, Marquis of Hartington, and from 1891
8th Duke of Devonshire. A man of great public eminence, he was
nevertheless shy and retiring by nature, and this photograph shows him in
unusually relaxed pose

learning played a very minor and sometimes non-existent part in their lives.

Spencer Compton was very shy by nature, and it took him some time to get used to being with so many other young men of his own age, and to accustom himself to their mode of living. But he soon developed a love of racing and gambling, although unlike many of his contemporaries he was always able to exert moderation when required. There were, too, plenty of opportunities for hunting and shooting, and as a result he found that he had 'very little time to read, and the day vanishes most unaccountably'. He obviously managed to do some work, however, as he left Cambridge in 1854 with a respectable second-class honours degree in mathematics.

Spencer Compton spent the next three years travelling abroad. First he visited Europe, where he tried hard to gain some appreciation of art in the galleries there. He wrote rather doubtfully to his father that 'perhaps a slight taste for pictures may be beginning to show itself', but despite all this the treasures with which he was surrounded, this early interest in art never reasserted itself. More to his taste was a ball at the Elysée Palace where he was presented to Napoleon III and, as he described it, 'to a host of swells', which resulted in his going to dine the following day 'with a female of that species, the Marquise de C——'.

In 1856 Spencer Compton went to Russia for the coronation of Alexander II, acting as a member of staff for his cousin Lord Granville, who was a special ambassador for the occasion. Apart from the endless presentations to members of the Imperial Family, which he found most tiresome, he thoroughly enjoyed his visit. He saw impressive reviews of the cavalry, attended State balls, and witnessed a splendid sham fight, which he reported gave 'a very good notion of a battle'.

When Spencer Compton returned to England in 1857 his inclination was towards politics, and so it was arranged that he should stand as the Liberal member for North Lancashire in the election of that year. He was returned without difficulty, and thus at the age of twenty-four began a career that was to last for fifty years, during which time he was regarded as one of the most able and popular politicians of his time.

He was not possessed of any great genius or exceptional political adroitness, but one of his characteristics was that he was totally without motives of personal gain, and as a result was able to look at problems with an unbiased eye. E. F. Benson, in his book *As We Were*, describes his virtues as a politician :

He had no axe to grind, and that was why he could deliver such stunning blows with it. His bitterest opponents could not accuse him of self seeking, because it was obvious that he wanted nothing for himself, for the man who in the course of nature will become the Duke of Devonshire and inherit colossal wealth and noble possessions has not very much that he can covet for himself among the vain trappings of the material world. So when, with his great position and very sound judgement, he made up his mind (which took time) on any political question, it was because he thought that such a course was right, and probity, when all is said and done, is the most valuable equipment in any career.

It is open to question, however, whether his talents would have been fully used if it had not been for the forcefulness and driving ambition of the lady who for thirty years was his mistress and who finally became his wife.

Born Louisa von Alten, a daughter of a German count, she came to England in 1852 as the bride of Viscount Mandeville, heir to the Duke of Manchester. She quickly established herself in English society. As a young woman she was extremely beautiful; Princess Catherine Radziwill saw her at a reception given by the Empress of Germany and recalls on being introduced to her 'how she struck me as the loveliest creature I had ever set eyes upon. Indeed I have only met three women in my whole existence who could be compared to her.'

It did not take long for her and her husband to become leaders of the 'fast set'. They were very popular with their own generation, and the Prince of Wales, no doubt impressed by this lovely woman ten years his senior, soon became a close friend. At Kimbolton, their country seat in Huntingdonshire, the Manchesters were able to provide just the sort of life he liked. Queen Victoria, however, disapproved strongly. Not only did the Duchess flaunt convention by such actions as walking around London unaccompanied, but she and her husband and the company they kept were just the sort of people whom the Queen feared would lead her

*Louisa von Alten, the German beauty who came to England to marry Viscount Mandeville,
heir to the Duke of Manchester. This very romantic portrait by Robert Thorburn
captures her good looks which were to thicken and coarsen with age*

son astray. She showed her displeasure by not inviting Louisa to the Prince's wedding, which was a cutting insult.

One amusing incident which took place in 1859 did nothing to lessen the Duchess's fast reputation, although it was hardly her fault. She was taking part in a paper chase, and while climbing over a stile caught a hoop of her dress in it and went head over heels. She landed on her feet, but her hoops and petticoats remained above her head. Lady Eleanor Stanley described the incident thus : 'they say there was never such a thing to be seen – and the other ladies hardly knew whether to be thankful or not that a part of her underclothing consisted of a pair of scarlet tartan knickerbockers (the things Charles shoots in) – which were revealed to all the world in general, and the Duke of Malakoff in particular'.

Louisa dutifully provided two sons and two daughters for the Duke of Manchester, but it was not a happy marriage. He was a wild fellow, for whom gambling played an important part in life. Louisa spotted the potential of Lord Hartington, and having decided upon her goal, she set out to capture him. Of course, there could be no question of divorce from the Duke of Manchester, but there would be no need for that anyway.

William Drogo, 7th Duke of Manchester and
Louisa's first husband, from a painting by Desanges

Provided certain rules were kept, and the correct protocol observed, the liaison could go ahead unhindered. She was well aware of the importance of keeping up appearances, and throughout her thirty years of friendship with Lord Hartington, although everyone knew about it the couple were never 'found out'.

Louisa's toughness of character and fierce ambition made her a fearsome opponent, and woe betide anyone who tried to oppose her. E. F. Benson described her as having 'something of a steam roller about her, neither kindly or unkindly, but crushing its way on and flattening out the unevenness of the road it intended to traverse'. She pushed and encouraged Lord Hartington, while doing all she could behind the scenes to forward his career. She was a bossy, controlling woman, but then that was what Lord Hartington needed, as by nature he was too lazy and easy-going to push himself.

The stories of his lethargy and somnolence are numerous. On one occasion he was asked why he so rarely spoke in the House of Lords, to which he replied : 'I can't refrain from yawning in the middle of my rare orations. I will go further. I fell asleep one afternoon, and dreamt that I was addressing an august assembly. By gad, when someone woke me up, I found that my dream was true, I was speaking to their Lordships.' On another occasion in the House of Lords, after having been asleep, he woke with a start, glanced at the clock and said, 'Good Heavens! What a bore! I shan't be in bed for another seven hours.' One morning when at home at Devonshire House, he was called by his servant at the usual time. But the Duke (as he was by then) looked out of the window and told his servant to go away, as he wasn't going to get up until the horrible fog had lifted. The servant returned two hours later, but received the same reaction from his master. At one o'clock the servant returned yet again, and on being told once more that it was too foggy to get up, the servant replied, 'I beg Your pardon Your Grace, but that is not fog outside, but the tent Her Grace has had put up for her luncheon party this afternoon.'

No society lady would have dared challenge Louisa's claim to Lord Hartington, as she wielded enough power to make or break almost anyone. In the early 1860s, however, a serious threat came from an unexpected quarter. Lord Hartington met and fell madly in love with a famous courtesan, Catherine Walters, known as Skittles. Skittles was no ordinary lady of easy virtue but a fascinating and beautiful woman who charmed all men who met her, and caused terrible jealousy among the society ladies. She had come to London from Liverpool, and became attached to a livery stable, where she learnt to ride extremely well. The owner of the livery yard realized that she could be an excellent advertisement for his business, and so he used to send her to Rotten Row, in a habit so tightly fitted that she had to be naked underneath, and mounted on his showiest hacks, which she would show off to perfection.

Catherine Walters, the famous courtesan known familiarly as 'Skittles',
who had a close liaison with the Marquis of Hartington. The affair ended
in 1862, when Hartington departed for the United States, and Skittles to
make her mark upon the Second Empire in Paris

Skittles caused a great stir in Rotten Row. Many of the ladies looked askance, covering their jealousy with disapproval, but the men were intrigued by this exquisite equestrienne. Lord Hartington's great passion for her was demonstrated by his lack of reticence and discretion, which was quite out of character. Mistresses of the demi-monde were normally provided with a little house in the suburbs, but Lord Hartington put Skittles in a house in Mayfair, and gave her beautiful horses and a life settlement which provided a generous annual income. He made no secret of his love for her, and openly appeared with her at society functions such as the Derby.

While this was going on, Louisa was much too clever to interfere. She carried on with her own busy life, and bided her time until a suitable moment arrived. She knew quite well that if Harty Tarty, as Lord Hartington was known, married Skittles, his career as a politician would effectively be over, and she guessed that underneath he, too, was aware of that.

Gossip about Lord Hartington and Skittles was rife in the summer of 1862, and matters came to a head after *The Times* and the *Daily Telegraph* published some articles about it. Skittles was referred to as Anonyma, and although Lord Hartington's name was not actually mentioned, everybody knew full well who was the subject of the articles, which were written in highly disapproving terms. Lord Hartington unwillingly agreed to take up the suggestion that he should go to America to gain first-hand knowledge of the Civil War which was then raging, while poor Skittles packed her bags and set off to Europe.

Lord Hartington was genuinely distressed at having to say goodbye for ever to his Skittles, and one cannot help feeling sorry for this kindly, retiring man, who because of the rules of the society in which he lived was forced to give up the girl he loved.

On his return from America six months later, Louisa knew that her time was ripe. She invited him for tea, and began talking to him about politics and his future plans, making no mention of Skittles and indeed ignoring completely the fact that she had ever existed. After the heartbreak that he had suffered, Harty Tarty must have felt pleased to find someone in whom he could confide, and who apparently loved him.

Shortly after this Louisa became his mistress, a position she never relinquished. He grew to love her very deeply, and she him, although partly due to the standards of the day, and partly through her character, she never showed him a hint of affection in public. Lady Warwick, however, wrote a revealing story in her memoirs about Louisa after she had become Duchess of Devonshire, which showed that she was indeed human.

She never relaxed, never revealed any emotion. She appeared neither angry nor pleased, nor vexed, though at times she would be strident, emphatic and persistent. As a hostess she was correct, cordial upon occasion, outspoken, but always unperturbed – except on one winter evening. My husband and I were staying at Chatsworth for a shooting party . . . the custom was for the guns to come in and join the ladies for tea, but for once they did not arrive, so we took tea alone. Afterwards we went our separate ways, and for some reason or other, I walked to the entrance hall. To my surprise I found the Duchess pacing up and down in a great state of agitation. 'Is anything wrong ?' I asked, and there was a note of real distress in her curiously guttural voice as she told me that she could not imagine what had happened to the Duke.

Naturally I suggested that it was some ordinary delay that had kept them, but she still strode restlessly to and fro and I could see tears in her eyes. At last the guns came in, the Duke leading them, and shaking the snow from his ulster.

'Why, what on earth is the matter ?' he enquired tenderly, and went on to explain that they had turned aside to look at some new buildings on the estate.

With Louisa behind him doing all she could to promote his career, Harty Tarty continued his work in politics that he had begun before his American tour. In 1863 he became Under-Secretary for War, and after the death of Lord Palmerston, he was promoted to Secretary of State. Despite his somnolence and apparent lack of enthusiasm, he gained an excellent reputation as a straightforward and honest politician respected by all as a result, in the words of Henry Asquith, the future Liberal Prime Minister, of his 'great insight into practical conditions, quiet and inflexible courage, and above all, tranquil indifference to praise and blame, and by absolute disinterestedness'.

Early in 1875, after the defeat of the Liberals by Disraeli, Gladstone announced his retirement from politics. Hartington was asked to fill the

Spy's cartoon of the Liberal Treasury bench, entitled 'Babble, Birth and Brummagem'. On the left sits 'Babble', the Liberal Prime Minister, W.E. Gladstone, celebrated for his powers of oratory. To Louisa's irritation, Gladstone was to make it impossible for Hartington, alias 'Birth', seated centre, ever to become Prime Minister, though he was Leader of the Opposition for a short time. 'Brummagem' is Joseph Chamberlain, one of the Birmingham Radicals, whose manifesto declared 'A Free Church, Free Land, Free Schools, Free Labour'

position of Leader of the Opposition and, goaded by Louisa, he unwillingly agreed. He did not have to remain there for long, however, as in 1878 Gladstone, by popular demand, was recalled.

In the election of 1880, the Liberals triumphed over the Conservatives, and Disraeli advised the Queen to send for Lord Hartington and to ask him to take office as Prime Minister. This she did, but Gladstone, peeved at being overlooked in favour of a man who had still been in the cradle while he, Gladstone, was making a name for himself as a politician, refused to serve under him.

Hartington was uncompromisingly against Gladstone's policy of Home Rule for Ireland, and as a result of this he began to make moves to break away from the Liberal Party. In 1886 he appeared on the same platform as Lord Salisbury, thus laying the foundation of the Unionist Alliance between the Conservatives and the dissident Liberals. Over ninety Liberals followed Lord Hartington against Gladstone's Home Rule bill, and as a result of this, when an election was called in 1886, the Unionists came to power. Lord Salisbury asked Lord Hartington to take office as Prime Minister, but he refused.

In December 1886 the Chancellor of the Exchequer, Lord Randolph Churchill, proposed a sweeping programme of reform, in which he suggested cuts in the armed forces. The Conservative Party was very shocked by this, and Lord Salisbury willingly accepted Churchill's resignation. This crisis shook the confidence and security of the Government. Lord Hartington was considered the ideal person to rebuild its strength, but when Lord Salisbury asked him for a third time to take office as Prime Minister, he once again refused.

Louisa must have been bitterly disappointed at never realizing her ambition of seeing Harty Tarty as Prime Minister, and as a fiercely ambitious woman herself, she must sometimes have felt very frustrated at his easy-going lack of drive. Despite his wealth and position in society, he was basically a simple man. When a colleague told him that the proudest moment of his life had been the occasion of his maiden speech in the House of Commons, Lord Hartington replied, 'The proudest moment of my life was when my pig won first prize at Skipton fair.' He was completely unconcerned about dress, and one of his hats became so worn and shabby that his friends clubbed together and started a fund from which they bought him a new piece of headgear each birthday. William Smith, the highly respected leader of the Conservative Party, met him in Aix-les-Bains and described him as looking like a 'seedy, shabby sailor'. Lord Esher, in his reminiscences, *Cloud Capped Towers*, described Lord Hartington's mode of living thus:

His lot was cast amid noble, even gorgeous surroundings, but he was not luxurious. The rooms he occupied were ascetic in their plainness. Although no-one looked more dignified when, blue ribboned, he stood with his Duchess at the head of the awkwardly winding staircase at Devonshire House, he dressed as a rule with extreme simplicity. He rose late and was seldom seen before 10 a.m. taking a meagre breakfast on a small table placed next to his uncomfortable escritoire. He stalked to bed in the small hours; generally after a game of bridge, which he played with vexatious deliberation and mediocre skill. He would leave the card room at the Turf Club only just in time to be late for dinner, however exalted the rank of his host. When a Marlborough House dinner was kept waiting, Hartington was invariably the cause of delay. His manner was a blend of curtness and courtesy. Perfectly at ease himself, he was often the cause of uneasiness in others. A certain hauteur which became him well had been grafted onto a naturally humble nature by the Duchess who had been at some pains to force him to tidy his unruly hair.

That he could on occasion be brusque is well illustrated by the following story. One day when in a railway carriage he was asked by another passenger whether he minded his smoking, to which polite question Hartington retorted, 'I don't mind if you smoke, if you don't mind if I'm sick!'

In 1890 the Duke of Manchester died, leaving Louisa free to marry Harty Tarty. He had succeeded to the dukedom in 1891, and on 16 August 1892, after a decent interval following the Duke of Manchester's death, Louisa finally became Duchess of Devonshire. She was held in great awe by everyone, for apart from the power she wielded, she could have an acerbic tongue for those who stepped out of line with her. On one occasion when a rumour was circulating that Devonshire House was to be sold, a friend asked her if this was true. She replied drily, 'Yes, perfectly true. We are proposing to live at Clapham Junction instead. So convenient a train service'.

Her servants, too, held her in respect. One day, while out for a drive in the countryside around Bolton Abbey, the Devonshires' estate in Yorkshire, she took her guests for a walk to see a local landmark. As she was getting back into the wagonette, one of the horses walked forward, as a result of which the Duchess was thrown on to her knees. Without a

'The Double Duchess' Louisa. For many years she was a leading social hostess as the Duchess of Manchester, and in 1892 she became the Duchess of Devonshire. This photograph, taken in the 1890s, shows clearly the strength and determination of her character: she was not a lady to be trifled with

word, she struck the coachman sharply across the back with her cane, and then sat down and calmly continued her conversation with her companions.

Louisa was feared and respected, and admired for certain qualities; but except for a few close friends, led by her loyal husband, she was not loved. Consuelo, Duchess of Marlborough, who evidently detested her, wrote how she had gone to Longchamp Races during the period of mourning after Queen Victoria's death, and finding the requisite black clothes depressing, she had donned a pair of white gloves. Unfortunately, the first person she met at the races was the Duchess of Devonshire, who delivered a furious lecture on her lack of respect for the late Queen. The

Duchess of Marlborough also referred to Louisa's looks, which had by now sadly deteriorated. 'Rumour had her beautiful, but when I knew her she was a raddled old woman, covering her wrinkles with paint, and her pate was a brown wig, her mouth was a red gash.' E. F. Benson, although less blunt, makes quite plain with his use of flowery simile her unsuccessful attempts to retain an appearance of youthfulness. 'Later she became the wraith of what she had been, and still be-wigged and be-diamonded and be-rouged, she was rather like the half ruinous shell of some castellated keep, with the flower boxes in full bloom on the crumbling sills.'

By 1897 Louisa was still as powerful a figure as ever in the worlds of society and politics. Known for obvious reasons as the Double Duchess, her energy and zest for life remained unabated. She continued attending balls and race meetings and entertaining at her husband's houses with indefatigable spirit. Each year they spent time in at least five different houses. From the middle of July until 12 August they stayed at their seaside home, Compton Place in Eastbourne. Then they moved up to Bolton Abbey in Yorkshire for the grouse shooting, where they remained until the middle of September. The winter months were spent at Chatsworth, in Derbyshire, where they entertained for shooting parties and for Christmas. The extravagance of these entertainments was, even for those days, great. Turtles, destined for soup, were sent up from London three times a week at a cost of £24 each, sometimes only to be thrown away unused. A Derbyshire farmer on being told the price of these reptiles exclaimed, 'I'm darned if that dead shell fish isn't worth as much as my dead cow!' Because there was always so much food left over, anyone who worked at Chatsworth by the day was allowed to take away enough food for his supper. This practice eventually had to be stopped, as non-workers from far and wide came for a free meal, and one man was seen removing wheelbarrows full of food.

In the early spring the Devonshires went to Lismore Castle in Co. Waterford, where their time was spent salmon fishing on the Blackwater River. By the middle of April it was time to pack up and move to Devonshire House in London for the season, which got under way at the beginning of May.

DEVONSHIRE House stood between Stratton Street and Berkeley Street and faced on to Piccadilly, with views over Green Park. The site on which it was built first came into the possession of the Cavendish family in 1697. The land had originally been occupied by Hay Hill Farm, but in 1665 Lord Berkeley, an officer in the Royal Army under Charles II, purchased this land as a site for his London dwelling. At this time it was still a comparatively sparsely occupied area, but by the 1690s it had become a fashionable part of town in which to live, and houses and sites were much sought after.

William Cavendish had been created Duke of Devonshire in 1694 as a result of his support for William III. A suitable London residence was required to match his elevated rank, and so when Berkeley House came up for sale in 1696, it was acquired by the Duke. There was some initial difficulty over the transaction, as the Marquis of Normanby equally desired the house, and indeed considered that he had bought it. The matter had to go to the House of Lords, and it was over a year until they 'after mature deliberation decreed it for the Duke of Devon'.

The Duke and his successors lived in Berkeley House, which became known as Devonshire House at the beginning of the eighteenth century, until 1733, when it was destroyed by a disastrous fire. While some alterations were in progress a workman allowed a pot of glue to boil over on the fire which was heating it, and the flaming liquid set alight the woodwork. Fortunately a platoon of guards was passing, and with their help many of the treasures were saved, including a *trompe l'œil* of a violin by John Van der Vaart (now at Chatsworth), a portrait by Tintoretto, and

Devonshire House, Piccadilly, in the early nineteenth century. The two drawings show the austerity of the exterior created by William Kent. The upper picture features the wide forecourt and jutting porch which protected guests from the elements as they alighted from their carriages. The lower drawing depicts the back of the house, set in spacious gardens. During the time of the 6th Duke, a semi-circular apse was added to the back elevation to house the circular 'crystal' staircase

most of the fine furniture and porcelain, though unfortunately it was not possible to save the wall paintings by Louis Laguerre.

After the fire, the 3rd Duke did not waste any time in planning a new residence, and selected William Kent as a designer. Kent was a Palladian architect who had made his name as the designer of the Treasury in London, as well as country houses such as Stowe and Holkham Hall. For the Duke of Devonshire he planned, as was his style, a house with a severe unadorned façade encasing a rich and luxurious interior.

Some critics considered the house too plain, and during the Victorian age, when elaborate and ornate designs were the fashion, it was little admired. James Ralph, an architectural critic and writer of the nineteenth century, said cuttingly of its elevation, 'It is spacious, and so are the East India's warehouses, and both are equally deserving of praise.'

The Saloon in Devonshire House in 1820, from a watercolour by William Hunt, showing the room after the 6th Duke's alterations. A photograph of the Saloon in the early twentieth century is reproduced on page 40

Devonshire House first became famous as a political centre in the time of the 5th Duke, who succeeded in 1764. He was a phlegmatic and rather uninteresting person who was remembered chiefly as the husband of the fascinating and famous Georgiana, Duchess of Devonshire. Everyone who knew her loved her; she was beautiful and sympathetic, and at a time when it was the fashion for women to affect boredom and ennui, she conquered London with her enthusiasm and zest for life. Charles James Fox won his election in 1784 as a result of her strenuous canvassing; it was in this campaign that originated the story of how she won a vote from a reluctant butcher by giving him a kiss, and where she received her favourite compliment, from a drunken Irishman who asked her to light his pipe from the fire in her beautiful eyes.

At Devonshire House she entertained on a large scale, and soon had gathered round her the brightest stars in the intellectual, political and fashionable firmaments. Alas, though, Georgiana was a compulsive gambler, and as she grew older, the beautiful rooms at Devonshire House were used more and more for long evenings of cards, at which she lost enormous sums of money. Georgiana died in 1806, and her husband married Lady Elizabeth Foster, who had lived with the Devonshires as a friend of Georgiana's and mistress of the Duke for some years. This union was only to last for a short time, however, as the Duke died in 1811 and was succeeded by his twenty-one-year-old son, William.

The 6th Duke made a number of structural alterations to Devonshire House. The entrance had originally been a double flight of stone steps arranged as an external staircase, which led straight into the reception rooms on the first floor. This was done away with, and the front door was instead put on the ground floor. A semi-circular apse designed by Sir Matthew Wyatt was built on to the back of the house, containing a circular staircase known as the 'crystal staircase' because of its crystal handrail. The 6th Duke also redecorated the house almost completely, leaving only his mother's little blue and white boudoir as she had had it, in memory of her.

The Bachelor Duke, as he became known after his death, loved drama and theatricals, and when in 1850 Charles Dickens and Sir Edward Bulwer-Lytton were trying to launch the 'Guild of Literature and Art',

The marble staircase, with its crystal handrail, at Devonshire House,
from a photograph taken in 1920, shortly before the house was demolished.
Guests at the Devonshire House Ball would have ascended these stairs to
join the receiving line

*In 1851, the Guild of Literature and Arts staged an amateur performance
of Sir Edward Bulwer-Lytton's comedy, 'Not as Bad as We Seem' at
Devonshire House, with Charles Dickens in the role of the poet Lord
Wilmot. The evening was attended by the Queen and Prince Albert, who
can be seen in the box*

the Duke offered them Devonshire House as a setting for their
fund-raising plays. In 1851 Bulwer-Lytton's comedy, *Not As Bad As We
Seem*, was first put on there in front of a distinguished audience including
the Queen and Prince Albert. Dickens appeared as Lord Wilmot, a part
which apparently did not suit him, as according to one onlooker he looked
more like 'the Captain of a Dutch Privateer'.

Devonshire House was ideal for entertaining. It had a large courtyard
in front with plenty of room for carriages to enter and turn, thus
facilitating the arrival and departure of guests. Many large houses in
London had their entrance directly on the street, and therefore when
entertainments were taking place traffic jams would build up in the street
outside and the guests would have a long wait both when arriving and
when waiting for their carriages to be called at the end of the party.

Behind Devonshire House there was a big garden, which in the
summer could be used by guests to wander in the fresh air away from the
crowds inside, or, if the size of the party was such, it could hold a
marquee. Gardens were always welcomed by party-goers, since at
'crushes', as big receptions were then known, the combination of large
crowds of people, stifling heat, and a long wait in the queue to be received,
proved for many quite an ordeal. Women had to suffer the extra
discomfort of tightly laced bodices, and fainting fits were not uncommon.

A few days before the Devonshire House Ball, Joseph Chamberlain had given a party at which the crush had been so great that Princess Louise, the fourth daughter of Queen Victoria who was married to the Marquis of Lorne, had been overcome and had nearly fallen underfoot. So dense was the crowd at this party that it had been impossible to clear a path for the Prince and Princess of Wales. The Prince was so angry that he left the party without even being received, much to the shame and embarrassment of his hostess.

Devonshire House, however, was on a big enough scale comfortably to contain a large crowd. A pillared entrance hall led through glass doors to the inner hall with its beautiful marble circular staircase, which wound round and up to the first-floor landing. The impression thus far was of an interior as severe in aspect as the exterior. The floors were of stone, and the only furniture in the entrance hall was a writing-table and two ancient-looking footman's chairs by the fireplace. The inner hall contained, apart from the staircase, only a huge marble basin on a pedestal.

The whole aspect changed dramatically once one reached the reception rooms on the first floor. The ballroom, which was the biggest room in the house, faced on to the garden at the back. It was a glorious room, with four long bay windows and a mirror between each one, which gave an illusion of even greater size. According to E. B. Chancellor, in his book *Private Palaces of London*, its 'elaborate gilding and ceiling decoration, in itself a thing to wonder at, reminded one of those Venetian Palaces in which colour is enriched by gold, and gold takes on a hundred shimmering tints from adjacent colour.' The walls were of yellow and white brocade, with the furniture upholstered in dark blue brocade in a gold framework. Two huge chandeliers of glittering crystal hung from the ceiling, with gold and crystal candelabras lighting up the walls. The floor was of polished parquet, and the heavy mahogany double doors, of which there were four sets, were highly polished and picked out in gold.

The saloon, which faced on to the courtyard, was equally magnificent in its decoration. Chancellor described it as like 'one of those gorgeous apartments which the wealth and luxury of Venice at its great period could alone conceive, and the pencil of Veronese was alone able to perpetuate'. He went on:

▲ THE MORNING ROOM   ▼ THE SALOON   ▲ THE GREEN DRAWING ROOM

▲ THE SALOON

▲ THE DINING ROOM   ▼ THE DRAWING ROOM

▼ THE SALOON

*All these photographs were taken in Devonshire House in the early part of the twentieth century, but they show
well the richness of the interior at the time of the 8th Duke. The Saloon in particular was lavishly decorated,
reminding one visitor of 'one of those gorgeous apartments which the wealth and luxury of Venice at its great
period could alone conceive'. The ceiling was painted in 'trompe l'oeil' to give the effect of immense height, and
was decorated with the Devonshire ducal coronet and badge of the snake, and, in the centre, the device and motto
of the Order of the Garter*

. . . the massive nature of the gilding and carving, the colossal mirrors framed on Brobdingnagian principles, the domed ceiling rich with painted wreaths and festoons of flowers and a thousand arabesques, in the midst of which the ducal coronet and crest is displayed, and the 'Cavendo Tutus'*, the Cavendish family motto, seems to take on itself another significance which has resulted from the systematic following of its advice.

All the Dukes of Devonshire had been enthusiastic art collectors, and by the time the 8th Duke succeeded there was a fine collection at Devonshire House. In the ballroom alone there was a portrait by Tintoretto, a Poussin, a Rubens, a Bassano and a Le Sueur, among many other lesser masters. Covering the walls of the other reception rooms were two Rembrandts, a Reynolds portrait of Lord Richard Cavendish, a Franz Hals, a Peter Lely, a Carracci and a Tintoretto. There were also many other pictures which were then attributed to great masters, but which have now been reassessed as being by the school of, or by someone else altogether.

As well as the paintings, there was a superb collection of Sèvres and Chelsea porcelain, and a large amount of fine French furniture of the Louis XVI and First Empire periods. As was the fashion in 1897, every reception room was crammed with as much furniture as it would hold, arranged for the most part in little groups of chairs and a sofa, often backed with a screen. Table tops and chimney pieces were covered in signed photographs and knick-knacks, while large ferns and palms were placed wherever there was space.

The walls in all the reception rooms were hung with heavy silks or damask, and the curtains were of a similar material, or of velvet, usually with elaborate pelmets. But the plaster work and carvings were so fine, and the pictures and furniture were of such quality, that the rooms of Devonshire House gave the appearance of elegance and beauty, rather than the heavy, ornate impression of so many Victorian interiors.

* Safety by caution. In fact the author is wrong : the ceiling carries the Garter motto.

EVERY season the Duchess of Devonshire gave a number of entertainments, including a dance which was held regularly each year on the night after the Derby.

The year of the Diamond Jubilee was obviously special, however, and the Duchess took the opportunity of adding to the celebrations by planning a ball to outdo all balls.

Fancy dress balls were extremely fashionable at the time, and indeed they had been a popular form of entertainment ever since dress became an important and telling item in the lives of men and women of fashion. At the court of James I there were many such entertainments, usually described as masques. Wilson, in his *Memoirs of the Reign of James I*, says that 'the court was a continued maskarado where the Queen and her ladies, like so many sea nymphs or Nereides, appeared often in various dresses, to the ravishment of the beholder, the King himself being not a little delighted with such fluent elegance as made the nights more glorious than the days'.

In 1575 Queen Elizabeth I had made a particularly memorable visit to Kenilworth Castle in Warwickshire to be entertained by her favourite, Robert Dudley, Earl of Leicester. On her arrival, she

was met in the park at a short distance from the first gate of the castle by a person representing one of ten sybils clad in a dress of white silk, who pronounced a proper poem in English rhyme and meter. This her Majesty graciously accepted, and then proceeded to the second gate where a porter, tall of person and wrapped also in silk, had a rough speech full of passions, in meter aptly made to the purpose. When the porter had concluded his harangue, six trumpeters clothed in long garments of silk who stood upon a wall of the gate sounded a tune of welcome while her Majesty rode along the yard into the inner gate. At her first entrance a floating island was discovered upon a pool, glittering with torches on which sat the Lady of the Lake, attended by two nymphs, who addressed her Majesty in verse, with a historical account of the antiquity and of the owners of the castle. Arion being summoned for the same purpose appeared on a dolphin four and twenty feet long, carrying within its body a whole orchestra. Then followed gifts presented by persons who represented mythical beings.

Queen Victoria and Prince Albert were fond of fancy dress balls, and in 1842 they gave a Plantagenet Ball at which they appeared as Queen Philippa and Edward III. The Queen looked especially striking, adorned as she was with a diamond stomacher – a jewelled bodice – estimated to be worth £60,000. In 1845 they gave a Royal Bal Costume, for which costumes had to date from between 1740 and 1750. It was by all accounts a splendid sight, although many of the guests tottered around in great discomfort, unaccustomed to the high heels fashionable in that period.

In 1851 the Queen and Prince Albert held a Restoration Ball, at which, according to E. S. Turner in his book *The Court of St James's*, 'although certain gents appeared as specific historical characters, no attempt seems to have been made by the ladies to identify themselves with the illustrious courtesans of Whitehall'. A fine example of Victorian moral standards.

In 1874 a famous fancy dress ball was given at Marlborough House in London, for which the decoration was arranged by the artist Sir Frederick Leighton. Fourteen hundred guests were invited, and the Princess of Wales, dressed as a Venetian lady, led the Venetian quadrille with the Marquis of Hartington. It is with this ball that the Devonshire House Ball has most often been compared.

In 1895 Daisy, Countess of Warwick gave a huge ball at Warwick Castle, choosing the reigns of Louis X V and Louis X VI as the theme for dress. That winter was particularly hard, and conditions were so bad that all building and construction work was brought to a halt, which increased the already high unemployment. Lady Warwick was greatly disturbed by the hardship and poverty surrounding her, but she consoled herself that the huge ball she planned would at least create employment for local decorators and dressmakers.

Daisy, Countess of Warwick, from a photograph taken in 1890

Two years before the Devonshire House Ball, Daisy held a magnificent fancy dress ball at Warwick Castle, taking as her theme the reigns of Louis XV and XVI of France. This drawing from 'The Graphic' shows some of the guests between dances. But Robert Blatchford, the editor of the Socialist paper 'The Clarion' was not so impressed, accusing the Countess of frivolity and wastefulness. Stung by his criticism, she stormed into his offices, only to be converted to the principles of Socialism

The ball was an enormous success, and Daisy was well pleased with her efforts until, a couple of days later, while reading the glowing reports in the newspapers, she came across an account in the Socialist paper, the *Clarion*, which damned the ball and her own utter wastefulness and frivolity. After all her good intentions of providing employment Daisy was mortified, and immediately stormed up to London and into the office of the paper's editor, Robert Blatchford, on whom she vented her fury over his grossly injudicious epistle.

Unprepared as he was for the sudden appearance of this fashionably attired, beautiful lady, Blatchford managed to calm her enough to talk to her about Socialism and explain that such work as she had provided was totally unproductive, and against all Socialist principles. Daisy was considerably subdued, and in her memoirs she claims that this conversation changed her outlook on life; from then on she dedicated herself to the study and practice of Socialism.

The Jubilee provided Louisa with the excuse she needed, while she herself was possessed of all the requisites for giving a grand ball. She had unlimited money, Devonshire House, one of the grandest houses in London, in which to give it, as many servants and helpers as she needed, and a boundless supply of energy. Her position in society was so powerful that she knew there would be no question of a rival ball on the same evening, but even if there had been, the Duchess's invitations were so coveted that it would not occur to anyone to regard her ball as second choice.

The Duke was, no doubt, resigned, even pleased with the idea. He knew that his wife would cope with all the organization, and that he had no fear of being pestered by her about plans for it. If the bustle of activity became too trying, he could always take refuge in his club, or retire to the House of Lords. He had an exceptionally phlegmatic attitude towards entertainments. On one occasion he was dozing in the Turf Club, when he was woken by a messenger telling him to return at once to Devonshire House, as the Prince of Wales had arrived and the Duchess was waiting to start dinner.

Having decided to make her ball fancy dress, Louisa had to choose a theme. Since fancy dress balls were so popular, many themes such as 'birds', 'flowers', and practically every historical period had already been used, and so finally she decided to give the guests wide scope for their imagination, and stipulated on the invitation that dress should be 'allegorical or historical costume before 1815'.

Although not mentioned on the invitation, it was suggested by the Duchess and others that there should be various courts and processions on different themes in which the guests could join. This was not compulsory, and indeed many guests preferred to keep their costumes a surprise, but the idea quickly became popular, and some of the guests got together beforehand and organized their outfits to harmonize as one group, while others had their costumes made independently but planned to join a procession at the ball.

There were five courts strictly arranged: the English Court of Elizabeth I, which was to be led by Lady Tweedmouth; the Austrian Court of Maria Theresa led by Lady Londonderry; Queen Guinevere and the Knights of the Round Table, with Lady Ormonde representing the Queen; the Court of Louis XV and XVI to be led by Lady Warwick as Marie Antoinette; and the Russian Court of Catherine the Great, headed by Lady Raincliffe. There were also three more loosely arranged groups; the Orientals led by the Duchess of Devonshire; the Italian procession; and the allegorical costumes.

As the weeks of the season went by and the day of the ball approached, signs that a big occasion was imminent became plain at Devonshire House.

Outside in the garden, workmen were erecting a huge marquee under the direction of a foreman and the Devonshire House comptroller, whose job it was to make sure that all the outside decoration and construction work was carried out correctly. Beside the marquee carpenters were busy hammering into place the temporary staircase that was to lead from it to the house, while around them were rolls of red carpeting waiting to be laid, and bundles of striped awning to be hung in the marquee and beneath the verandah. Elsewhere in the garden the beds were being weeded and the paths regravelled, while the head gardener made a careful inspection to see that nothing was left undone, for the garden had to be in as perfect order as the house for the night of the ball.

Inside the house the staff were busying themselves with preparations. Each of the servants would have had his or her particular task laid out, for the hierarchy from housekeeper and steward to scullery maid and odd job man was clearly defined and discipline strict below stairs. Unfortunately we have no account of the preparations for the Devonshire House Ball from the servants' point of view, as all the household accounts for this period are missing from the family archives and the Duke's secretary destroyed all his personal papers when Harty Tarty died in 1908. But it is highly likely that servants would have been called in for the occasion from Chatsworth and the other Devonshire houses. This army of helpers was under the overall control of the house steward, though the housekeeper was directly responsible for the female staff.

The housekeeper, aided by two secretaries, was put in charge of affairs inside, having been given precise orders from the Duchess on how the house was to be arranged. Because of the large number of guests, caterers and extra servants were hired and the Duchess, assisted by her secretary, spent a whole day with the managers of the catering firm deciding on the menu and how the supper was to be organized. Fortunately the kitchen at Devonshire House was large enough for the preparation of the food, but a small tent was erected outside to serve as a pantry, to facilitate the serving of supper.

There was also the mammoth task of organizing costumes for all the servants, as the Duchess had decided that every one, from the cloakroom maids to the head butler, should be in fancy dress. The servants hired from outside were to be dressed in Elizabethan and Egyptian costumes from a theatrical outfitters. Each member of the Devonshire House staff was to have a specially made costume, provided by the Duchess: the men-servants were to be dressed in the blue and buff Devonshire livery of the eighteenth century, the maids in Elizabethan sprigged frocks. Again, sadly, no photographs of these costumes have survived.

The picture archives at Chatsworth contain very few photographs of the Devonshire household in the nineteenth century. This photograph is the only surviving record of servants at the time of the Devonshire House Ball, and shows footmen in their livery of blue and buff, relaxing over a game of cards. The incongruous appearance of an Oriental carpet in an open air scene shows it was a very carefully posed group

Louisa herself chose M. Worth, the famous Parisian couturier as the designer and maker of her costume. Although he designed hundreds of dresses for fashionable women all over the world, he never seemed to fall short of ideas and could always be relied upon to produce something highly original as well as beautiful. The Duchess had chosen to portray Zenobia, Queen of Palmyra, and Worth designed a marvellously elaborate gown to match this exotic title. Margot Asquith considered the Duchess's choice of character to be most unrepresentative of her, as she thought the name Zenobia, Queen of Palmyra, evoked someone beautiful and romantic. The Duchess was neither.

Louisa was, in common with many women of this time, of large stature, but such was M. Worth's talent that he made her look imposing and stately, rather than obviously fat. The outfit was most striking, for as hostess the Duchess naturally wanted to create as great a sensation as possible. The dress had an under-robe of cloth of silver, wrought all over with silver thread and diamonds, with an over-dress of gauze shot with green and gold, embroidered to the waist with green and gold metal work decorated with jewels. Attached to the shoulders was a long train of turquoise velvet studded with jewels of all colours, and embroidered in gold in an Eastern design. Her ample bosom was contained in a bodice of gold cloth and lace, which was fitted over a whalebone corset into which her waist was laced as tightly as possible.

The whole outfit was enhanced by a lavish amount of jewellery, of which the Duchess possessed large quantities, as apart from the vast Devonshire collection, she had brought with her a considerable amount from her first marriage.

———————— * ————————

The hostess of the Devonshire House Ball: Duchess Louisa as Xenobia, Queen of Palmyra. Why she selected such a theme is not known, and as she was a heavy stout woman, the choice was incongruous. Nevertheless, the celebrated Parisian couturier, Monsieur Worth, used all his skills to produce a costume that was stately and striking. The advantages of being a Double Duchess are evident in the lavish amount of jewellery that she wore

THE DUCHESS OF DEVONSHIRE
as Zenobia, Queen of Palmyra

THE DUKE OF DEVONSHIRE, KG
as The Emperor Charles V

[52]

On her dress were strung literally festoons of precious stones, falling over the bodice and from shoulder to wrist on the arms. On her head she wore a gold band studded with jewels below two high branching diamond ornaments. Attached to these were ropes of superb pearls which fell down in loops over her ears, and from the back of her head right down on to her dress.

The Duke was less ostentatious in his choice of outfit. He chose to go as the Holy Roman Emperor, Charles V, and his costume was copied from the portrait of that monarch by Titian. It was an apt choice, for not only did he look dignified and every inch the *grand seigneur* but also, as *The Times* commented, the costume highlighted the curious similarity between the Cavendishes and the Hapsburgs. The Duke, of course, like the Emperor, owned great treasures and a vast acreage of widespread lands. Despite the large array of jewels at his disposal, however, he retained his simplicity, and the only decoration that he wore was a genuine badge of the Order of the Golden Fleece which was lent to him by the Prince of Wales.

———————— * ————————

The Duke of Devonshire chose to represent the sixteenth-century Hapsburg Holy Roman Emperor, Charles V, and copied his costume from Titian's famous portrait. It is not known whether he particularly admired the Emperor, but contemporary accounts of the ball were quick to make comparisons between the Hapsburgs and the Cavendishes

R ARELY had a social event created such a stir of anticipation as the Devonshire House ball. Since the beginning of May, when the season began, it had been the principal topic of conversation among the members of society, and to receive or not to receive an invitation became a matter of burning importance. The approval of the Duchess was the seal of approval and acceptance in society, and her approbation resulted in recognition and invitations for many who might otherwise have remained in comparative obscurity. An invitation to the fancy dress ball confirmed membership of the 'smart set', and was therefore much sought after. Apart from this, everyone was eager to witness what promised to be one of the most lavish spectacles of the century; since it was the main subject of interest that season, everyone wanted to have the fun and excitement of preparing for it, and to join in the discussions on the all-absorbing question of what to wear, or to have the fun of trying to keep their outfits a secret while at the same time trying to discover what the others were wearing.

Society, as already observed, was less clearly defined than it had been twenty years before. Jewish financiers like the Rothschilds and the Sassoons, and rich industrialists such as Arthur Wilson had been 'accepted' through the Prince of Wales. These men were able to provide the kind of life that His Royal Highness enjoyed – sport and gambling and entertaining on a grand scale – and consequently people who would not have been considered acceptable earlier in the century were invited to the great houses of London. Some members of the 'old school' were most distressed to find people whom they considered upstarts welcomed to the

The Prince of Wales had cut a swathe through social conventions by befriending Jewish financiers and rich industrialists. 'The Times' went so far as to accuse him of hobnobbing with 'American cattle-men and prize fighters'. But the Prince continued to enjoy the companionship and financial acumen of men such as Ernest Cassel and Alfred Beit, both of whom attended the Devonshire House Ball. Cassel LEFT, *a clever financier who gave Edward sound advice on monetary matters, went to the ball as the Spanish painter, Velazquez. Beit* RIGHT, *who had made a fortune in the South African diamond trade, chose to represent Frederick Henry of Nassau*

Devonshire House Ball, while they themselves were not invited. Daisy, Lady Fingall, wife of the State Steward of Ireland and a leading figure in Irish Society, was one such, and it is said that she never forgot and never really recovered from the disappointment.

Invitations were sent out on the last day of May, only a month before the ball. Some of the guests were well enough acquainted with the Duke and Duchess to know that they would receive an invitation, and many had their outfits already planned (though there was at least one such hopeful who, confident of being asked, had ordered an expensive outfit only to wait in vain for an invitation). Those who had waited in the hope of being asked, and had been lucky, quickly began to get themselves organized.

Dressmakers and designers were very busy that summer, driven to distraction with orders and counter-orders. Messrs Nathan of Coventry

Street and 'Alias' of Soho Square, who were leading suppliers of theatrical costumes, each provided over one hundred outfits, the latter supplying the Prince of Wales, his younger brother, Arthur, Duke of Connaught and his Duchess, his son, George, Duke of York, and other members of the Royal Family. Many of the ladies were dressed by two well-known couturiers, Mrs Mason and Mrs Nettleship, who must have been under enormous pressure. With every guest trying to outdo the others in magnificence and originality, an immense amount of work had to go into the making of each dress, perfection being demanded in every case.

The excitement and concern about deciding what to wear was on an unprecedented scale. Lady Randolph Churchill describes in her memoirs the weeks preceding the ball.

Great were the confabulations and mysteries. With bated breath and solemn mien a fair dame would whisper to some few dozen or more that she was going to represent the Queen of Cyprus of Aspasia, Fredegonde or Petrarch's Laura, but the secret must be kept. Historical books were ransacked for inspirations, old pictures and engravings were studied, and people became quite learned in respect to past celebrities of whom they had never before heard. The less well known the characters, the more eagerly they were sought after. 'Never heard of Simonetta ? How curious, but surely you remember Botticelli's picture of her, one of the beauties of the Florentine Court ? No ? How strange . . .'

Some guests chose to go as one of their ancestors : Lady Eva Dugdale, for example, was dressed as her great-aunt Lady Anne Bingham, and the Marchioness of Granby went as Mary Isabella, Duchess of Rutland from a miniature by Cosway. Others, such as Lady Beatrice Herbert whose dress was copied from the Gainsborough portrait of Signora Bacelli, searched the art galleries for inspiration. The Print Room at the British Museum, normally occupied by serious students, was suddenly invaded by smart ladies and gentlemen leafing through the prints and drawings.

Once a costume had been decided upon, the next step was to ensure accuracy of detail, to which great care and attention was devoted. Lord Ronald Leveson-Gower, in his book *Records and Reminiscences*, describes how Lady Garvagh came to him anxious for information about a dress of the Louis XVI period. He lent her some prints and photographs from his

*Many of the guests at the ball took a famous painting as
their theme for their costume. Lady Beatrice Herbert,
daughter of the Earl of Pembroke, selected Gainsborough's
portrait of Signora Bacelli (inset), and modelled her
costume on the eighteenth-century original*

*The current mistress of the Prince of Wales at the time of the Devonshire House Ball
was the Hon. Mrs George Keppel, who attended as Madame de Polignac. Taking great care
to ensure every detail of her costume was correct, she even managed to secure material that was
made in the eighteenth century. No photograph exists of the lovely Alice Keppel in her
ballgown, but this print of her was based on a painting by Roberts*

collection for which, he says, she was 'quite unnecessarily grateful'. Alice Keppel, the mistress of the Prince of Wales at the time of the ball, also wore a dress of the period of Louis XVI. It was a beautiful gown, with full panniers of rose and silver brocade and a full hooped petticoat in silver cloth, the latter embroidered in tinsel threads of all shades forming a design of roses and lovers' knots in long lines from waist to hem. Not only was every detail of the design correct, but Mrs Keppel had managed to procure material that was actually manufactured in the eighteenth century.

Another guest, who was as keen on making a sensation as being accurate, seriously considered hiring an elephant from London Zoo as a means of transport to the ball in keeping with her Eastern costume. She was only dissuaded when the zoo keeper warned her that the beast might not be as placid as usual if faced with the Piccadilly traffic.

Many of the guests owned fine collections of jewels, and some went as far as to have them reset so as to match the period of their costume. Those without enough real jewels bought artificial ones, and Oriental pearls were bought in ropes so that they could be knotted and knotted and still fall to the ground. Others went to the Parisian Diamond Company in Burlington Arcade and hired crowns and other jewels for the evening.

The hairstyles were of course most important. In those days ladies' maids were skilled in the art of hairdressing and normally arranged their mistresses' hair, but for the ball such elaborate and unusual styles were adopted that experienced coiffeurs were needed to create them. On the day of the ball every hairdresser in London had been requisitioned, and some had even been brought over from Paris. So much in demand were they that some ladies had to have their hair done first thing in the morning, and were thus unable to move all day for fear of disturbing their coiffures.

Every conceivable hairstyle was represented. The ladies wearing a costume from the period of Louis XVI or eighteenth-century England had their hair powdered and curled, while the men wore periwigs. Ladies dressed in Elizabethan costumes had to have their locks teased into the tiny curls that were the fashion in those days. Others more fortunate, such as Dante's Beatrice, Dido, Queen of Carthage, and many of those from the court of King Arthur and Queen Guinevere, enjoyed what must have been a rare opportunity to wear their tresses loose and flowing. Lady Lurgan and Lady Sophie Scott, however, felt unable to break the bounds of convention even for this occasion, for although they represented the Furies they wore hairnets to keep their hair tidy.

Head ornaments of every description were worn; those who had suitable tiaras wore them, and some ladies whose tiaras were not of the right period for their costume had them reset in an appropriate style. Many people, including Lady Essex who went as Berenice, Queen of Palestine, had a crown in the shape of a peacock's tail made specially for the occasion, while the Countess of Minto, representing Princess Andrillon, wore a jewelled wimple snood. Ostrich feathers and plumes were very popular, especially with those in costumes from the French Courts, and Lady Alice Montagu, as Petrarch's medieval Laura de Sada, had bunches of orchids in her hair which gave an effect as striking as any of the jewels. Margot Asquith chose a coiled sequinned snake as the

Lady Sophie Scott took her inspiration from classical mythology and attended the ball as a Fury. As this photograph demonstrates, there was little abandonment in her image. Even her hair was kept carefully under control with a hairnet

Lady Alice Montagu, one of the twin daughters of the 8th Duke of Manchester and Consuelo Yznaga, chose an early fourteenth-century theme as Petrarch's Laura de Sada. She used orchids rather than jewels for her headdress

The New York beauty, Adela, Countess of Essex, as Berenice, Queen of Palestine, with a crown in the shape of a peacock's tail, a triumph of art nouveau jewellery

The Hon. Mrs Reginald Talbot as a Valkyrie. Her Wagnerian headdress proved entirely unsuitable for the evening, giving her a bad headache, and no doubt making it difficult to negotiate doorways

headpiece of her outfit as an Oriental snake-charmer, which was typical of her attitude to life, in that she preferred making an outrageous impression rather than one of beauty.

Some of the guests sacrificed comfort in their desire for accuracy. The Hon. Mrs Reginald Talbot, dressed as a Valkyrie, complained that her metal winged helmet gave her a bad headache, but she did not dare take it off lest she was unable to do up her hair again.

Some of the men were even more excited and exacting about their costumes than the women. Lord Dunraven considered the reason for this to be that, whereas women could adorn themselves as brilliantly and

THE DUKE OF MARLBOROUGH

as the French Ambassador at the Court of Catherine of Russia

elaborately as they wished in everyday life, men were very restricted in their dress, and so a fancy dress ball gave them the opportunity to gratify their desire for more flamboyant clothes.

The Duke of Marlborough went straight to Paris to have his costume designed and made by M. Worth, one of the leading couturiers of the day. The outfit he demanded was so elaborate that even M. Worth was taken aback by the extravagance. In his autobiography he declares that

. . . although the shop in the rue de la Paix had seen a number of freak orders taken, this request from the Duke that we make him a costume for the DHB, a request that he would not hear of us denying, was something new under the sun that shone on the Worth establishment. However, we acceded to his demand after a few scandalized protestations, and got to work on a Louis XV costume of straw coloured velvet embroidered in silver, pearls and diamonds. The waistcoat was made of a magnificent white and gold damask that was an exact copy of a very rare old pattern. Each pearl and diamond was sewn on by hand, and it took several girls almost a month to complete this embroidery of jewels. Had the Duke not insisted that his costume be perfection, we should never have dared put such costly work into it. In spite of his orders about elegance, when I came to make out his bill, I was almost afraid to begin it. But at last when I got it totalled it came to 5000 francs.

A huge sum in those days, for an outfit for one night's engertainment.

The men also used great resourcefulness and ingenuity in deciding upon and procuring their costumes. There is a story that on the first night of *Lorenzaccio*, a play by Alfred de Musset about France during the Renaissance, a well-known member of society presented himself at the stage door of the Adelphi Theatre, and handing in his card requested to see Sarah Bernhardt, who was playing the leading role. Once in her

--------------------- * ---------------------

Charles, 9th Duke of Marlborough as the French ambassador at the court of Catherine II of Russia. He was a strong contender for the most extravagant costume at the ball, commissioning Worth to produce an outfit covered in pearls and diamonds, and costing the princely sum of 5000 francs

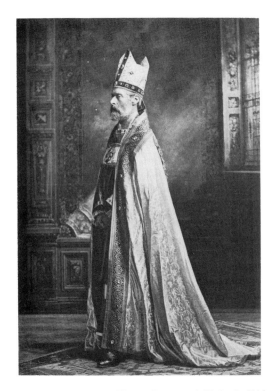

Lord Rowton chose to represent Thomas Cranmer, the Tudor Archbishop of Canterbury, and took part in the procession of the Elizabethan Court. Lord Rowton was particularly interested in alleviating the lot of London's poorest inhabitants, and Rowton Houses still care for the homeless

dressing-room, he begged to be allowed to copy exactly the male costume that she wore in the production. This she agreed to, and at his request promised not to breathe a word about it to anyone. At the close of the second act, a dashing army officer came to the actress's dressing-room and asked permission to copy the outfit. Madame Bernhardt gave her consent, but kept her promise to her first visitor. As he took his leave, the Hussar captain asked her to keep his plan a secret, which she again agreed to do. At the end of the play a young baronet appeared at the stage door, needless to say with the same request. Sarah Bernhardt of course granted his wish, and swore not to mention it to a living soul. So each young man duly had his outfit prepared, and arrived at the ball well pleased with himself for his ingenuity and looking forward to the impression he was going to make – only to find two other fellows clad in identical costumes.

Some of the men dressed as characters with whom it seems likely they identified. Lord Rowton, a philanthropist who financed Rowton Houses for down-and-outs, went as Archbishop Cranmer, while Henry Asquith, later Lord Oxford and Asquith, went as a Roundhead soldier. The latter's costume was apt because he tended to be puritanical in his outlook on life and did not approve of the extravagant living standards of many of his contemporaries. Indeed, unlike the majority of London society, Asquith was not at all keen to attend the ball. His wife Margot, who was a very gay, high-spirited lady, was determined to go, however, and in her autobiographical book, *Off the Record*, she describes how she managed to persuade him.

Asquith: 'What do you suppose I could dress in ?'

Margot [*reflecting*]: 'Go as a Roundhead soldier.'

Asquith: 'Oliver Cromwell ? That would be ridiculous and a presumption on my part.'

Margot: 'No, not Cromwell, but one of his soldiers. You are made for the part. It will be a unique occasion, and ever so grand!'

Asquith: 'I don't care to be dressed up. I have to make an important speech in the House of Commons the day after the ball. I detest what you call "unique occasions", nor do I care much for grandeur.'

> *At this I interrupted him, and said that since no one was likely to dance, we could leave the ball early, which would give him ample time to prepare his speech.*

Asquith: 'I can only make a short speech when I have prepared it. Long speeches bore everyone.'

Margot: 'Anyway, you know that you can speak very well on every occasion. Do take me to Devonshire House. You have not forgotten that you promised that you would make every effort to take me out with you. Have you forgotten this ?'

Asquith: 'No. I made you this promise. But you don't expect that I shall enjoy myself, do you ?'

Margot: 'Yes, I do. I insist upon it. You must always enjoy yourself when we are alone together!'

Asquith: 'Alone, yes – but not in company.'

Margot: 'Never mind. You need never go to a fancy dress ball again. But just to please me, go to this one.'

THE EARL OF ROSEBERY

as a gentleman of the XVIIIth Century

Mrs Asquith managed to persuade her husband to go, albeit unwillingly, because he was conscious of being older than she was and he had a horror of being a kill-joy and preventing her from enjoying herself. Once he had given his consent, she had to get to work immediately on organizing his outfit, as there were only ten days to the ball and she was determined that he should look perfect in his part. She must have been successful for her husband was reported as looking 'most convincing'.

Lord Rosebery, one of Asquith's predecessors as Liberal Prime Minister, went as a gentleman of the eighteenth century, and was most upset that in all the newspapers he was given the wrong attribution. 'I was described, greatly to my disgust, as that effeminate gossip Horace Walpole. If challenged for a name I should have given the Duke of Devonshire for that time. But I had no idea of anyone.'

Reginald Brett, later Viscount Esher, who had been private secretary to the Marquis of Hartington, was rather priggish and took himself very seriously. Although he appears to have been embarrassed at the idea of dressing up, the interest he took in his outfit suggests that he was as concerned as everybody else about being a success at the ball. At the beginning of June he mentioned in a letter to a friend that he had found a fancy dress, 'all black velvet and trimmed with beads and a ruff! And long silk legs in which I suppose I shall look as big a tomfool as everyone else – or more so'. On 18 June he wrote again, saying that he had tried on his costume which he went on to describe. The actual dress was satisfactory, but he decided that he needed a dagger to complete the outfit and sounded most concerned because he 'did not know where to get a good one'. By the time the day of the ball arrived, however, he had clearly become tired of all the fuss that was being made about it, and his feelings were summed up in a letter he wrote on the day : 'Tonight is this infernal ball. I will tell you all about it tomorrow. I expect it will be a fiasco.'

---- * ----

Archibald Primrose, 5th Earl of Rosebery, as an eighteenth-century gentleman.
At the time of the Devonshire House Ball he was Leader of the Liberal Opposition to
the government of the Marquis of Salisbury. He was considerably put out at the
ball at being mistaken for 'that effeminate gossip, Horace Walpole'

Reginald Brett, who became 2nd Viscount Esher in 1899. He had acted as the Marquis of Hartington's private secretary from 1878 to 1885 and was to serve as a close and influential adviser of Edward VII. He lovingly, but deprecatingly, described the making of his costume as a gentleman of France in letters to a friend, 'all black velvet and trimmed with beads and a ruff. And long silk legs in which I suppose I shall look as big a tomfool as everyone else – or more so.'

Some of the people who had been looking forward so keenly to the ball were prevented from coming at the last minute because of a death in the family. In the nineteenth century mourning had a strict protocol, and its rules had to be carefully observed. Black had to be worn, and under no circumstances could those in mourning attend balls or any sort of entertainment. Maurice Baring, the diplomat and writer, suffered the bereavement of his maternal uncle shortly before the ball was due to take place, and so despite the complicated costumes that he and his family had had made, and their anticipation that had been building up for weeks, none of them was able to go. On the very day of the ball, when excitement was reaching a pitch, nine-year-old Marjorie Cavendish, daughter of Lord and Lady Chesham, died as a result of a riding accident, thus preventing her parents, her grandparents the Duke and Duchess of Westminster, her uncle and aunt, Lord and Lady Ormonde and their daughter Lady Beatrice and Lady Constance Butler from attending.

Mrs Hwfa Williams, a much loved figure of the day, described by Lady Augusta Fane as a 'landmark of Edwardian Society', suffered a similar disappointment. She was one of the people prevented from going to the ball by the death of her sister-in-law, Lady Aylesford. Fifteen years earlier, Edith Aylesford had been the centre of the Aylesford scandal, in which she had threatened to elope with Lord Blandford while her husband was on a tour of India with the Prince of Wales. On being informed of this Lord Aylesford returned from India, demanding a divorce from his wife and a duel with Lord Blandford. Lord Randolph Churchill, Blandford's brother, concerned that a divorce would cause an even bigger scandal, attempted to blackmail the Prince of Wales into preventing it by threatening to publicize some flirtatious notes which the Prince had written to Lady Aylesford some years before.

The Prince of Wales refused to intervene, but Lord Aylesford was persuaded by his friends not to go ahead with the divorce. There was no reconciliation with Lady Aylesford, however, who as a result of the scandal was ostracized from society and forced to live as a virtual recluse. She finally got her revenge by dying when she did, thus preventing some of the members of her family who had so willingly shunned her from attending the ball.

Poor Mrs Hwfa Williams was bitterly disappointed. Her autobiography, *It Was Such Fun*, contains a vivid description of her preparations for the ball, followed by the cruel anticlimax :

The Devonshire House Ball was the greatest fancy dress ball that I have ever seen, although I had heard of the wonderful fancy ball at Marlborough House which took place before I came out [1874]. It was the year of the Diamond Jubilee, London was at its fullest and there was a spirit of festivity in the air.

All the Duchess's friends were to take part in this ball, and neither expense nor ingenuity was spared in devising and carrying out the most beautiful costumes. Old books and costumes were consulted to make sure that the historical figures were accurate in every detail, and in many cases those taking part assumed the characters of famous ancestors.

For my part, the Duchess asked me to arrange an Italian Quadrille. Lord Lathom and Lord Peel who had both been Lord Chamberlains were to appear as Doges of Venice; Helen d'Abernon and Alice Montagu, one of the lovely twins of

Consuelo Manchester, Lord Alexander Thynne and Lord Wimborne were in my Quadrille. I was to represent Caterina Cornaro, with Ivor Wimborne as my King of Cyprus. We used to go twice a week for rehearsals and what fun we had at them! As in amateur dramatics, rehearsals for Quadrilles are often the best part. All was going splendidly, and we were worked up to a pitch of excitement when two days before the ball was due to take place, Hwfa's sister, Edith, died. The Duchess came round to see me at once to see what we should do. I had been taking such an interest in the arrangements of the Quadrille that it was perfectly impossible to drop it, though of course it was equally out of the question that I should go to the ball myself. There was anxiety as to whom should take my place, but kind Lady Plymouth kindly saved the situation by taking my part. Deeply disappointed as I was, it was some satisfaction to me to know that the part I had been looking forward to and rehearsed so fully would be carried out by her, as she is so artistic and looked so lovely.

The night of the ball I dined at Arlington House where a dinner party was being given for all members of my Quadrille. It was very tantalizing to see them all in their costumes, and to know that they were going to have such a lovely time. However, we all went off to Devonshire House where Frank Mildmay, who was also in mourning, took me upstairs to a skylight on top of the staircase, from which we could look down onto the ballroom. Never shall I forget the heat we endured as we stood at our observation post. We stayed there until nearly four in the morning, abandoning it only for a few moments to creep down the back staircase to get something to eat. How I longed to be down in that room! I had thought of nothing else for so long that it was most disappointing; but very sad was Edith's death for all her sisters.

. . . Never in my life have I been so tantalized as I was that night at my spy hole in the skylight, and the longer I looked the more I wanted to go down among them all.

THE week before the ball was a time of considerable pressure for the Duchess. Not only did she have all the organization and last-minute arrangements to see to, but she had also to try to cope with queries from anxious guests who were not sure about some detail or other for their quadrille. A large amount of publicity had preceded the event, and it was already being described in the newspapers as the ball of the century before it had even taken place, so Louisa must have felt a little uneasy in case it should not live up to exvectations.

Then, during the five days preceding the day of the ball, two incidents took place which must have caused almost unbearable strain even for so tough a character as Louisa. On Tuesday came a report that her sister was seriously ill with a complaint that could prove fatal. This put Louisa in an agonizing position, for if her sister were to die before Friday, under no circumstances could the ball take place.

The news quickly spread, and it was suggested that if her sister did die, the ball could perhaps be held in another house, such as the Duke and Duchess of Sutherland's Stafford House, or Londonderry House, the home of Lord and Lady Londonderry. But that would have been small consolation to the Duchess of Devonshire; to have sat at home in mourning while the ball was held in another house would have been a cruel blow indeed.

The other incident took place on Wednesday, 30 June. The Duke had gone to the races at Newmarket, no doubt partly to have a break from all the activity at Devonshire House, and as he was being driven from the racecourse to his house in the town, his carriage horse fell, upsetting the vehicle and causing all the occupants to be thrown out. One of the Duke's companions had to be taken to hospital, but by a stroke of luck the Duke escaped with no more than a shaking.

One cannot help feeling sorry for Louisa having such worries on top of all the other pressures as a hostess. But after what must have seemed the longest week in her life, Friday eventually arrived. No messenger had called with news of her sister's death, the Duke was safe and well after his mishap. Devonshire House was ready and the marquee was up, as servants and attendants bustled round making final preparations.

Most of the furniture in the reception rooms had been removed and stored away, the chairs being placed round the edge of the ballroom. As every bit of space was required, the Duke and Duchess had decided to make available their own suite of rooms at the end of the house to be used as extra reception rooms. The parquet floor in the ballroom had been polished until it gleamed. The huge chandeliers had been taken down and each piece of crystal washed and polished before being fitted with new candles.

Early in the morning vast quantities of plants and flowers, accompanied by several gardeners, arrived by train from Chatsworth. Having spread dust-sheets around the rooms the gardeners set to work, hanging the flowers in festoons, and arranging them in huge vases and in banks against the walls.

Finally, by early afternoon, the house was ready. Now the kitchen became the centre of activity, as the caterers, under the eagle eye of the Devonshire House chef, chopped and sliced and prepared the delicacies for supper. Next door to the kitchen, the servants' hall was being prepared as a refreshment room for visiting coachmen.

Throughout the morning the Duchess had been going from room to room supervising the last-minute arrangements, nodding her head in approval, or asking for some detail to be changed. Nothing escaped her eye, and she expected absolute perfection. Finally Louisa was satisfied that everything possible had been done. After lunch, with a last glance around the empty reception rooms, Louisa, accompanied by her maid and a hairdresser, went to her bedroom to begin the lengthy process of preparing herself for the Devonshire House ball.

[72]

*The front of Devonshire House at the time of the ball. The wide forecourt
enabled guests to arrive in their carriages without causing the tremendous
traffic jams that so often bedevilled large social occasions*

AT eight o'clock on the evening of 2 July, excitement over the ball was at a high pitch. Right up until the last moment odd articles of fancy dress were being delivered : hansom cabs flew up and down the streets of Mayfair and Belgravia carrying wands and staffs, feathers and flowers, while guests impatiently awaited their arrival, anxious lest their vital accessories should not arrive in time.

Some of the unlucky ones not invited to the ball hurried from house to house to catch a glimpse of their friends dressed up in their finery, while maids and hairdressers added the final touches to costumes and coiffures. Those already dressed were driving out to dine at the different houses where dinner parties were being given before the ball, and onlookers would have seen some marvellous sights as the carriages bore the strangely dressed guests to their destinations.

---
*

One group of close friends that attended the ball in force was the Souls. Consuelo, Duchess of Marlborough described them as 'A brilliant company, a select group in which a high degree of intelligence was to be found happily allied to aristocratic birth.' One of the leading ladies of the circle was Ettie Fane, who married William Grenfell in 1887. She attended the Devonshire House Ball as Marie de' Medici, Queen of Henry IV of France. She is seen in this group portrait with the Hon. Sir William Harcourt (seated centre) and A.J. Balfour. Sir William was a leading Liberal MP who eventually became Chancellor of the Exchequer. For the ball he chose to represent one of his ancestors, Simon, Lord Harcourt, who was Lord Chancellor in 1710. Arthur Balfour, known as 'King Arthur' by his Souls' friends, was an immensely successful Conservative, rising to the premiership in 1902. According to the Duke of Portland he was embarrassed by his fancy dress as a gentleman of Holland, though he seems quite happy in his guise in this photograph

THE Rt Hon Sir W. V. HARCOURT, MP

as Simon, Lord Harcourt, Lord Chancellor, 1710

THE Rt Hon A. J. BALFOUR, MP *as a gentleman of Holland*

MRS GRENFELL *as Marie de' Medici*

Lord and Lady Tweedmouth gave a dinner party for those who formed the Elizabethan procession, and Lord and Lady Arlington entertained those in the Italian Court. At their house in St James's Square, Lord and Lady Cowper gave a dinner composed largely of 'the Souls', a group of intelligent and artistic men and women who had reacted against the typically society lifestyle of gambling, illicit love affairs and sporting activity which they despised. The Duke and Duchess of Portland, the Marquis and Marchioness of Granby, Sir Edgar and Lady Helen Vincent, Henry and Margot Asquith, George Curzon and Arthur Balfour were among the Souls at this dinner. Arthur Balfour, normally an uninhibited person, was apparently overcome with embarrassment in his outfit of a seventeenth-century Dutch nobleman, and according to the Duke of Portland he 'arrived rather late and tried to creep along the wall behind everyone else.' Edith Chaplin, who was to become the Marchioness of Londonderry, described in her autobiography her experiences at the dinner party.

I sat next to the late Lord Oxford and Asquith, dressed as Oliver Cromwell. [He was not, in fact, Cromwell, but a Roundhead soldier.] He looked perfect in the part, and, I remember was very kind to me. We must have been a strange contrast; the austere Puritan with close cropped hair, and Elaine the Lily maid of Astolat carrying Sir Lancelot's shield, with hair hanging loose, only bound with a fillet – I had an immense quantity of deep yellow colour, long enough to sit on. It got into Mr. Asquith's way during dinner as well as my own! The dinner party was very large and we were somewhat crowded for space.

---
*

Four members of the Souls in their Devonshire House Ball costumes. ABOVE LEFT :*the Duchess of Portland – her striking good looks evident in this photograph – went as the Duchess of Savoy.* ABOVE RIGHT :*Ettie's husband, William Grenfell, attended as Mercutio from Shakespeare's 'Romeo and Juliet'.* BELOW LEFT :*Lady Helen Vincent, considered to be the prettiest woman in England, as a Genoese lady in the style of Van Dyck.* BELOW RIGHT :*Violet, Marchioness of Granby, who became Duchess of Rutland in 1906, chose an outfit based on Cosway's portrait of one of her husband's ancestors, Mary Isabella, Duchess of Rutland. A highly skilled artist, she drew portraits of many of the Souls and exhibited regularly at the Grosvenor Gallery. She passed her very fine looks on to her daughter, Lady Diana Cooper*

At Devonshire House a large crowd of spectators had gathered as early as half past nine, all anxious to get a good view of the spectacle. The house was brilliantly lit, the Piccadilly side of it illuminated by a large crown flanked on either side by the letters V.R. and enclosed in a wreath. The courtyard was lit by gas lamps, while the windows were all ablaze from the brightly lit interior.

The invitations were for half past ten, and most guests arrived in good time, anxious not to miss a moment of the great occasion. The spectators, restrained by policemen, craned their necks to see the arrivals, who were greeted with cheers and clapping, especially such popular figures as Lord Lonsdale and Lord Rosebery. One guest who arrived in a sedan chair was almost mobbed by a curious crowd as he passed down Piccadilly, and had to be assisted by two gentlemen in evening dress. Many members of society who had not been invited collected in the courtyard, and according to the *Daily Mail*, a relation of royalty was recognized in the crowd by a member of the Royal Family.

One of the earliest arrivals was Mr George Wyndham MP, dressed as the Emperor Johannus Palaeologus on his state visit to Venice in 1438. Another punctual guest was Viscount Peel as a Venetian doge, his crimson robe with its ermine tippet and the peculiar pointed cap being well adapted to his appearance. Lord Robert Cecil followed in black velvet, then several Roundheads in armour, on curiously friendly terms with some of Prince Rupert's cavalry, in their red coats embroidered with gold and large jackboots. Then came a Napoleon in the traditional uniform of the Petit Caporal, dark green coat and red facings, with a white waistcoat and breeches; after him came Antony escorting Cleopatra whilst conversing with a number of Queen Elizabeth's yeomen. By eleven o'clock there was a seemingly endless stream of carriages rolling into the courtyard in quick succession, depositing their load and then passing on to wait in an adjoining street.

Inside the house the scene was one of brilliance. The hall where the guests assembled as they waited to be received was a mass of flowers and greenery. The marble basin was filled with water lilies and ferns, and festoons of flowers hung from the staircase. The observant or botanically minded would have noticed among them the Night-Flowering Cactus, an exotic plant whose flowers come out only at night, the blooms lasting a few hours before dying by morning.

To the strains of the Blue Hungarian Band seated at the foot of the stairs, guests greeted each other with exclamations of surprise and admiration as they slowly made their way up the marble staircase. Henry Irving made a particularly impressive entrance according to one guest, who told Ellen Terry that 'as the cardinal swept up the staircase, his long train held magnificently over his arm, a sudden wave of reality seemed to sweep upstairs with him and reduce to pettiest make-believe all the aristocratic masquerade that surrounded him'.

Everyone had stories to exchange about the difficulties and amusing incidents that had occurred during their preparations for the ball. Some of those in outfits of thick material or armour were already regretting that they had not chosen costumes requiring a lighter stuff, while others in elaborate head-dresses were hoping and praying that they had been securely fixed and would not tumble to the ground whilst they made their curtsey to the Royal Family.

At the top of the staircase stood the host and hostess. Before them a Master of Ceremonies dressed in Elizabethan costume took the name of the guests and the characters they represented, and in a loud voice announced them to the Duke and Duchess. They were solemnly greeted, the Duchess sometimes making a comment on their costumes, while the Duke stood beside her, smiling patiently but no doubt looking forward to the arrival of the Royal Family, after which his duty of receiving would be over.

The arrival of Lady Londonderry was greeted by a murmur of admiration from the other guests. She represented Maria Theresa, Empress of Austria, and was, according to her daughter-in-law, a 'magnificent sight'. Her dress of white satin embroidered with several shades of gold and seed pearls was both beautiful and authentic to the period, but her jewels were overwhelmingly spectacular. Her stomacher was solid with diamonds and her train was held in place with two enormous sapphire and diamond brooches, while her powdered hair was crowned with the 'family fender', as she called the famous Londonderry tiara. With her magnificent jewels and her air of arrogant hauteur she was

THE MARCHIONESS OF LONDONDERRY
as Maria Theresa

ideal for the part of the Empress, and indeed one reporter remarked that 'so glorious was her costume, so regal her bearing that surely Queen Maria Theresa herself could not have outshone her'.

Although considerably younger than the Duchess of Devonshire, Lady Londonderry was the Duchess's one rival for the position of leading social and political hostess of the day. Aided by her beauty and her husband's fortune, she had forced her way up primarily by her incredibly strong and dominating character, which is strikingly described by E. F. Benson in his book *As We Were* :

She liked violence and strong colour, and sweeping along with her head in the air, vibrant with vitality. She did not plot, plan or devise, she went for life hammer and tongs, she collared it and scragged it and rooked it like a highwayman in a tiara, trampling on her enemies as if they had been a bed of nettles – and occasionally getting stung about the ankles in the process – incapable of leniency towards them, or of disloyalty to her friends. She did not want to forgive her enemies nor did she want any peace conferences with them : she hated them with a genial sincerity, and loved her friends without reserve.

Like the Duchess of Devonshire, Lady Londonderry was the driving force in her marriage. Lord Londonderry was a pleasant easy-going man who, although dutiful in his obligations, had neither the same energy nor the ambition of his wife. In 1886 he accepted the post of Lord-Lieutenant of Ireland, and while Lady Londonderry entertained magnificently at the Vice-regal Lodge, her husband when entertaining officially at Dublin Castle cut down the length of dinners to half an hour : if guests tarried too long over one course, their plates were whipped away before they had finished.

--------------------- * ---------------------

The Marchioness of Londonderry as Maria Theresa, the eighteenth-century Empress of Austria. Lady Londonderry was Duchess Louisa's one great rival as a social hostess, and like her possessed a forceful personality. According to E. F. Benson, Lady Londonderry 'went for life hammer and tongs . . . like a highwayman in a tiara'. Again, like Louisa, she made full use of her family jewels to enhance her costume for the ball, with a stomacher encrusted with diamonds and the famous Londonderry tiara, which she dubbed the 'family fender'

In 1902 Lord Londonderry became President of the Board of Education, a post in which his wife took a great interest. Sir Almeric Fitzroy, the Clerk of the Privy Council, gives an amusing account of a conference in which although Lord Londonderry was 'nominally a party to the conference . . . he remained at the end of the table in isolated dignity while Lady Londonderry held the Permanent Secretary and the subordinate official immediately concerned in close communication'. Apparently those present at the meeting were enormously impressed by her Ladyship's competence and grasp of the subject, but as Sir Almeric commented, 'It is certainly a new departure when a minister's wife undertakes to look into matters of departmental administration in the very seat of her husband's authority, and leaves him to the simple functions of an interested party.'

Lady Londonderry was very beautiful, and though some considered her face too arrogant for perfect beauty, she had no shortage of admirers. When the Shah of Persia first set eyes on her he wanted to buy her, and although that offer was refused, she was not averse to followers. At her home, Wynyard in County Durham, she had her bedroom on the ground floor and left the window permanently unlocked so that the gamekeeper could visit her whenever he so wished, and her youngest son Reginald was commonly acknowledged to be the son of her brother-in-law, Lord Helmsley. Poor Reginald was partially disabled, said to be as a result of Lord Londonderry hurling him to the ground in a fury on discovering his true paternity. This is only hearsay, however, and such an action would certainly have been quite out of character for the mild Marquis.

In 1884 Lady Londonderry embarked on her most famous love affair, the dramatic story of which has been immortalized in Vita Sackville West's novel *The Edwardians*. Lady Londonderry fell in love with Harry Cust, an exceptionally handsome and charming man whose attraction for the opposite sex was already well known. He was a member of the Souls, and his many love affairs caused him to be known after his death as the 'Father of the House of Lords'.

Cust, not content with Lady Londonderry alone, also took up with Lady de Grey, who was then the recently widowed Lady Lonsdale. Lady de Grey soon began to suspect that she had a rival for Cust's attentions, and so having let herself into his flat with the key that he had given her she searched the rooms for evidence, which she found in the form of some highly compromising love letters from Lady Londonderry. Lady de Grey took these letters, which included unflattering references to Lord Londonderry, and amused herself and her friends by reading out passages from them, before giving them to a servant to deliver to the Marquis. As a result of this, the story goes that Lord Londonderry never spoke to his wife again except when keeping up appearances in public, but in fact, although it took him a long time to get over the terrible hurt and humiliation that he had suffered, eventually he forgave her, and they remained close friends until his death in 1915.

It is easy to see that Lady Londonderry was in her element at the Devonshire House Ball. The photograph of her as Empress Maria Theresa does not contradict Lady Fingall's description of her as having 'the proudest face I've ever seen', and judging by her haughty expression and condescending smile, it is no wonder that she was held in such awe.

Lady Londonderry's rival, Lady de Grey, was hardly less striking in her costume, jewels and beauty. Regy Lister, a younger brother of Lord Ribblesdale, wrote in a letter describing the ball, 'The person who shone out conspicuously above everybody was Lady de Grey. When she walked up the room as the head of the Orientals – swathed in gold and clinging orchids on her head, and a long glittering train carried by an Arab slave, the effect was dazzling; one felt that she should always be dressed like that and never in nineteenth century clothes.' She represented Cleopatra, and showed great ingenuity in having a Nubian slave in real old Egyptian slave's attire to bear her train. Lady de Grey's beauty was of a quality that, according to E. F. Benson, made other women beside her appear 'a shade shabby. They wanted a touch of the sponge or duster'. She was very tall, but carried herself with such grace and poise that rather than looking too tall herself, she made other women appear squat.

Apart from beauty and a love for Harry Cust, Gladys de Grey had little in common with Lady Londonderry. She took no interest in politics, nor did she have any desire to entertain on a grand scale in a huge London house. She was subtle and refined and never tried to impress people with lavish displays of wealth or to seek publicity in any form. She would have been horrified had her parties been written up and described in detail by the press as were Lady Londonderry's.

She was married first in 1878 aged nineteen to the 4th Earl of Lonsdale, a cruel and thoughtless man with whom she was most unhappy. He went away fairly often on long cruises, and to begin with forbade her to invite any of her friends to stay in his absence. Later he changed his mind in case she should use this as an excuse to go and stay 'at all sorts of fast houses'. But he ordered that any friends she might ask be forbidden to ride his horses, shoot on his land, attend any local functions, or even use any of the reception rooms which would be kept locked in his absence. She herself was not permitted to stable any of her horses at home, and if she did so he declared that they would be removed to a livery stable for which she would have to pay. It must have been a blessed release to Lady Lonsdale when she was widowed less than four years later.

In 1885, shortly after the Harry Cust affair, she married Lord de Grey, and from then on dedicated herself to the regeneration and reorganization of the opera at Covent Garden. By the 1880s opera in London was no longer the great and fashionable institution it had been in the fifties but Lady de Grey managed, with tremendous energy hidden under an apparently casual exterior, and her exquisite taste, to revive it until such artistes as the de Reszke brothers and Nellie Melba were playing to packed houses.

———————— * ————————

Gladys, Countess de Grey, as Cleopatra and leader of the Oriental procession. She made a spectacular entrance in the ball in her shimmering costume with orchids on her head and in her corsage, and her long train held by a Nubian slave. She was a rival to Lady Londonderry for the amorous attentions of Harry Cust, a leading member of the Souls but not invited to the ball – possibly because of his scandalous reputation

COUNTESS DE GREY

as Cleopatra

Her husband, who became the Marquis of Ripon in 1909, did not share her love of the arts, being almost entirely preoccupied with sporting matters. Although he was Liberal MP for Ripon between 1874 and 1880, he is remembered primarily as being the finest game shot of his day. On one occasion at Sandringham he accounted for 28 pheasants in 60 seconds, and Lady Augusta Fane remembers seeing him kill a bumble-bee with a tiny 'collectors' rifle. Gladys de Grey was as uninterested in her husband's shooting activities as he was in opera, and she disliked having to entertain his shooting parties. This was partly because she found them boring, but also because the pressures of formal entertaining sometimes became too much for her. According to Margot Asquith, the smallest hiccup in her arrangements would make her almost hysterical. 'When anything went wrong with her entertainments – cold plates, a flat soufflé or someone throwing her over for dinner – her sense of proportion was so entirely lacking that she would become almost impotent from agitation and throw herself into a state of mind only excusable if she had received the news of some great public disaster.'

Lady de Grey was far more at ease at Coombe, her house in Wimbledon, where she was able to indulge her penchant for Bohemian society. She would invite opera singers such as Melba and Caruso as well as a few close friends, and give delightful informal parties with music and singing. It says much for her charm that she could persuade these artistes to sing in such impromptu fashion, as they very rarely made appearances at private concerts, and then only for a colossal fee.

When the Great War broke out, Lady de Grey distinguished herself in her management of a military hospital, which she no doubt enjoyed, as she was passionately interested in people and in discovering all she could about life. As Lady Augusta Fane described her, 'She had a fine character and a broad outlook on life. She had however, one fault, and that was an overwhelming curiosity to know everything and experience everything, and this inquisitiveness led her into dark places and amongst undesirable people, but fortunately it never altered or debased her mind.'

Lady de Grey attended the ball with her husband, who had also made a considerable effort with his costume. He went as Admiral Coligny, in a complicated outfit consisting of a black satin doublet slashed on the breast

Earl de Grey, who chose to attend the ball as Admiral Coligny, the sixteenth-century French Huguenot leader. His ornate costume was of black and yellow satin, and around his neck he wore a blue moiré ribbon carrying a cross

with yellow satin and puffed with lemon yellow satin edged and embroidered with black jet. The sleeves were also slashed and puffed in yellow satin, and over his shoulders he wore a black satin cloak lined with yellow, looped and braided with jet *passementerie*. His trunks were of black satin, puffed and slashed in the same way as the doublet, while on his head he wore a black velvet toque ornamented with gold and jewels, and round his neck a blue *moiré* ribbon holding a cross.

When Lady de Grey's first husband, Lord Lonsdale, died he was succeeded by his younger brother Hugh. Hugh Lowther, described by Lord Ancaster as 'almost an emperor, not quite a gentleman', was in every way different from his unpopular elder brother. Hugh was enormously popular with the British public, and when his yellow landau, drawn by two high-stepping chestnuts, drew up at the entrance of Devonshire House and he and his wife alighted in their outfits representing Sir Richard Lowther and the Countess of Essex, they raised the biggest cheer of all from the crowd that had gathered to watch the spectacle.

The death of the 4th Earl had come at an opportune moment for Lord Hugh; as a younger son he had received only a small allowance, and he seemed incapable of even trying to keep within it. He was further hindered by having lost what capital he possessed in a disastrous investment in cattle in America. However, he was saved from bankruptcy by the death of his brother, for on succeeding he inherited Lowther Castle in what was then Westmorland, Barleythorpe, a fine hunting box in Rutland, and a big London house in Carlton House Terrace, as well as a large yearly income from land and coalmines.

His first action on succeeding to the earldom was to enlarge his stable, which he did, like everything else, on a grand scale. His carriage horses were invariably chestnut and had to meet very exacting measurements in height and girth, and his carriages, of which he bought a fleet, were all painted yellow. With the footmen and coachmen also dressed in yellow livery he thus earned himself the sobriquet of 'the Yellow Earl'.

Lord Lonsdale loved animals, with which he had great affinity, and nothing was considered too good for his own. Whenever he travelled overnight by train he would have one first-class sleeper reserved for himself and one for his dogs. In the stable yard at Lowther (where every morning his coat of arms was etched out in the sand in coloured chalks) any sign of slackness or ill temper shown towards the animals meant instant dismissal for the offender.

The Yellow Earl was a great sportsman, especially in the fields of racing, hunting and boxing. His prowess at boxing was such that in his twenties he took on and beat John L. Sullivan, the world heavyweight champion, in a secret match in New York, and throughout his life he never hesitated to make use of his boxing skills if he considered the situation required it. When he was judging the costers' turnouts at the International Horse Show one of the costers complained about not winning, at which Lord Lonsdale swiftly knocked him out, much to the delight of the crowd.

Society was always a little doubtful about him, for he did not bother to observe the conventions. At the races he was as happy in the Silver Ring (the cheapest enclosure) as he was in the Members' Enclosure, and he was on familiar terms with all the less salubrious characters in the racing world. On one occasion, a friend had his tie-pin stolen at the races. He turned to Lord Lonsdale for assistance, who immediately sought out a thoroughly disreputable villain who ran a racecourse gang and got the tie-pin returned.

The one great sadness of his life was that he had no children. His wife had suffered a miscarriage after a hunting accident, as a result of which she was unable to conceive. Her general health too was ruined, and she was rarely able to attend balls or evening receptions. On this occasion, however, not even the prospect of having to spend several days in bed afterwards could keep her from the Devonshire House Ball.

The Countess of Lonsdale as Frances, Countess of Essex in the reign of Elizabeth I. Her husband, Hugh Lonsdale, the Yellow Earl, was one of the great outgoing personalities of the 1890s, but she was obliged to lead a quiet secluded life because of a hunting accident that ruined her health

THE Rt Hon HENRY CHAPLIN, MP

as Marshall Lefebvre

Another popular public figure who attended the ball was Henry Chaplin, a friend of Lord Lonsdale and, like him, a keen sportsman. Unlike Lord Lonsdale, Chaplin was perhaps the epitome of what was considered in the nineteenth century to be an English gentleman. E. F. Benson described him as 'a type that has never existed anywhere except in England, and will never exist there again, and he might have sat body and mind alike for a national statue of John Bull'. Although at the time of the ball Chaplin was in serious financial difficulties, this did not prevent him from having a splendid costume made for his representation as General Lefebvre. The outfit was in blue and gold, with every detail correct, and he made a magnificent figure as he walked up the stairs to greet his host and hostess.

Chaplin was born in 1840, the son of a parson, who at the age of nineteen inherited his uncle's estate at Blankney in Lincolnshire. It was at Oxford that he met and made a lifelong friend of the Prince of Wales, with whom he shared a love of racing and extravagant living. Hunting he pursued with such enthusiasm that at one point, while Master of the Burton, he kept four packs of hounds and hunted six days a week. His passion for this sport never left him, and even during his later years, when he weighed around eighteen stone, there were few to match him across country.

A staunch follower of Disraeli, Chaplin was an able politician, and in the general election of 1868 he was returned to Parliament unopposed as the Conservative member for mid-Lincolnshire. He continued to hold this seat until 1906, when he was defeated in the great Liberal victory. In the following year he was returned at a by-election for Wimbledon, in which he defeated Bertrand Russell by a majority of seven thousand.

———————— * ————————

Henry Chaplin as Marshal Lefebvre, one of Napoleon's leading generals. The epitome of an English gentleman, according to E.F. Benson 'he might have sat body and mind alike for a national statue of John Bull'

He was throughout his life a great force in county constituencies where, accompanied by his agent and a magnum of champagne, he would drive in his dog cart from one meeting to another, to be greeted by cheers from the farmers and country people with whom he was so popular and whom he understood so well.

At the age of twenty-four Chaplin had been the innocent party in one of the most notorious scandals of the Victorian age. He had become engaged to Lady Florence Paget, a high-spirited beauty known because of her tiny stature as 'the Pocket Venus'. A few days before the wedding was due to take place, Lady Florence went shopping, ostensibly to purchase some final accessories for her trousseau. She went to Marshall & Snelgrove in Oxford Street, and having gone in through a side entrance she emerged at the Oxford Street door, where the Marquis of Hastings awaited her with a cab and a licence. They were married at a church a few hundred yards away.

Henry Chaplin knew nothing of this until he received a note from Lady Florence after the ceremony had taken place. One can only imagine the pain and humiliation he must have felt, and although his hurt and anger killed his love for the Pocket Venus, the exposure to his friends' pity must have been torture to the proud man.

Lord Hastings and Henry Chaplin had already been rivals on the turf, but after he was married, Hastings developed an obsession about Chaplin's horses, and would back heavily against even his most fancied runners. This obsession reached a crescendo when, in 1867, Chaplin's colt Hermit was entered with high hopes for the Derby. A fortnight before the race, however, the horse broke a blood vessel, and it seemed unlikely that he would run, let alone win. But his trainer somehow managed to keep him fit, and Chaplin who believed in his horse backed him heavily, while Lord Hastings, encouraged by the news of the broken blood vessel, continued to back against him, including a large wager with his owner.

On Derby Day itself, the rumours about Hermit's health as well as a freak blizzard that was blowing, resulted in the colt's starting price going out to sixty-six to one. Neither did his appearance induce confidence: his coat was thick and staring, and in the paddock he looked far from a Derby winner. Lord Hastings was supremely confident as the field went down to the start, but alas for him, Henry Chaplin's faith in his horse was justified. Battling through the sleet and snow, brave Hermit got up to win by a neck.

This victory won Henry Chaplin about £140,000 and lost Lord Hastings £120,000, £80,000 of which was owed to Chaplin. Chaplin at this time showed his extraordinary generosity of character, for he not only never pressed Lord Hastings for payment, the debt being eventually discharged, but he did all he could to comfort and befriend Lady Hastings who was by now unhappy and disillusioned, her beauty and gaiety worn away by the depravity and dissipation of her husband.

In 1887 Chaplin married Lady Florence Leveson Gower, with whom he was extremely happy until her death in 1892. They entertained on a lavish scale and Henry continued to extract the maximum enjoyment out of life, in such an extravagant manner that the Duke of Westminster remarked, 'When our Henry is broke, which is only a matter of time, all the crowned heads of Europe ought to give him £100,000 a year in order that he may show them how to spend their money.'

Alas, the Duke's prophecy came all too true. Henry's magnificent hospitality and general extravagance plus dwindling land returns drastically reduced his fortune, and in 1897 Blankney and its estate, which was already heavily mortgaged, was sold to Lord Londesborough.

Behind Henry Chaplin in the queue to be received was Georgina, Countess of Dudley, who in her day had been one of the acknowledged beauties of Europe. With the exception of Lillie Langtry, no one during the second half of the nineteenth century aroused the same excitement and attention: wherever she went crowds would collect and people would stand on chairs to catch a glimpse of her. She was very tall, with lovely red-brown hair and a flawless complexion. A poem of typical Victorian sentiment describes her during the height of her fame:

> First Lady Dudley did my sense enthrall
> Whiter than chiselled marble standing there
> The Juno of our earth divinely tall,
> And most divinely fair.

At the time of the Devonshire House Ball, Lady Dudley was fifty-one, but age could not alter her lovely features, and her beauty was still most apparent. She was dressed as the Queen of Sheba, in a white and silver satin dress and a pale blue mantle wrought with gold; ropes of pearls covered her neck and bodice, and she carried a gold diadem set in turquoises and diamonds.

She had married a man nearly thirty years older than herself, but she adored him, and when in his latter years he became an invalid she cared for him with genuine devotion. He was a most eccentric person with many strange fads. Whenever his wife gave birth he would take to his bed and refuse to get up for several days. When he had a shooting party on his estate in Worcestershire, he would insist on his guests going out for the day's sport clad in morning coats and ordinary shoes, rather than the customary tweeds and hobnailed boots. He also had an aversion to black dresses; no member of his family was allowed to wear mourning, and any lady coming to one of his parties in a black dress would be asked to go away. Lady Augusta Fane tells the following amusing story about Lord Dudley. While he was on a visit to Paris, a friend whose wife was expecting a baby asked him to bring back a layette. Lord Dudley obliged, but so as to avoid the surprise of his valet at such articles; he hid it inside the trousers he was wearing. When he got to the customs and was asked if he had anything to declare, he lost his head, and clutching at his undergarments replied, *'Mais non, mais oui, mais si, j'apporte ici quelque chose pour faire plaisir à ma femme.'* *'Passez, Monsieur,'* replied the official. *'Il ne faut pas se moquer de la douane.'* Lord Dudley died twelve years before the ball, which is a pity since no doubt had he been alive he would have given his eccentricity full rein when choosing an outfit.

———————— * ————————

The Countess of Dudley as Queen Esther, in a flame-coloured dress with a stole of rich embroidery. As a young girl her beauty had attracted the painter, Sir John Millais, who used her as one of his models in his painting, 'Spring (Apple Blossoms)', in 1856

[94]

THE COUNTESS OF DUDLEY
as Queen Esther

Lady Dudley was accompanied to the ball by her son and daughter-in-law, the 2nd Earl and his Countess. Young Lady Dudley, who was dressed as Queen Esther in a flame-coloured gauze dress and a jewelled head-dress, was also beautiful; as a girl she had been painted by Millais, the central figure in his picture *Apple Blossoms*. Her husband, who came to the ball as an Italian courtier, loved shooting, and like his father went about it in a somewhat eccentric manner. Whenever he went out shooting, even when staying away with friends, he insisted on being accompanied by a large entourage including the head gamekeeper from his estate, a footman, two chauffeurs and his Austrian hairdresser who acted as loader. The Duke of Portland, on observing the cavalcade one day, described it as looking like 'a whole crowd of people going to the Derby'.

The entrance of Millicent, Duchess of Sutherland, with her sister, Sybil, Countess of Westmorland, excited much admiration, and the effect they made was all the more striking for its simplicity. Lady Westmorland, as Hebe, wore plain white draperies but had a huge stuffed eagle poised on her shoulder. She made a perfect picture, although moving freely was rendered very difficult by the eagle, and as she stood on the crowded staircase waiting to be received she had some anxious moments lest the bird should be knocked off in the crush. The Duchess of Sutherland, although the possessor of famous jewels, came very simply dressed as Charlotte Corday in a plain scarlet crêpe de chine frock and mob cap, the only adornment being a tricolour rosette. But her beauty was such that it needed no enhancement, and in many of the contemporary descriptions of the ball she is mentioned as having looked outstanding.

The Duchess, like her half-sister Lady Warwick, was a hostess of some repute, and she used her London home, Stafford House, to its full advantage. When her husband succeeded to the title in 1892 she relaxed the austere rule of the two previous Duchesses, and besides giving big receptions and balls, she was hostess at delightfully unconventional salons to which actors, artists and people of all nationalities were invited. Everyone who came was encouraged to show off his or her individual talents, and it was at one of these salons that Constance Stuart Richardson, a daughter of Lord Cromarty and a dancer in the style of

Sibyl, Countess of Westmorland, who based her representation of Hebe, goddess of youth and cupbearer to the gods, on a painting by Sir Joshua Reynolds. She was to find the huge stuffed eagle perched on her shoulder a considerable encumbrance during the evening of the Devonshire House Ball

THE COUNTESS OF WARWICK
as Marie Antoinette

[98]

Isadora Duncan, made her début. Her beautiful figure and immaculate dancing met with great enthusiasm, and it was largely due to this that she was sufficiently encouraged to appear in public.

The Duke of Sutherland, however, did not share his wife's enthusiasm for entertaining. Lady Fingall, in her autobiography *Seventy Years Young*, gives an amusing story about meeting the Duke at one of his wife's receptions :

He hated parties, and at those wonderful ones that his wife gave he wandered around like a lost soul. One night when I had just seen Sir Frank Swettenham, a famous ex-governor of Malay come into the room escorting a beautiful lady, I asked the Duke who the lady was. He stared at me.

'My dear Lady! It's no use asking me. You must ask Millie. I don't know who anyone is. Why, I hardly know who you are!'

The Duchess's half-sister, Daisy, Countess of Warwick, was a controversial figure in society in the 1890s. She had many friends and admirers, but because of her disregard for certain sacred conventions and her Socialist sympathies, she also had many enemies. Her Socialist ideals did not prevent her from attending the Devonshire House Ball (or indeed any other social occasions), at which, according to the magazine *Vanity Fair*, she appeared in 'triumphant beauty'. She wore her Marie Antoinette costume that she had originally worn at her own fancy dress ball two years earlier, and described thus in *Vanity Fair* :

———————— * ————————

Daisy, Countess of Warwick, wore her Marie Antoinette costume, made for her own Warwick Castle Ball two years earlier. Despite her newly adopted Socialist principles, she continued to enjoy parties and balls, and her lavish costume of velvet, satin and brocade and her fine jewellery would suggest a certain amount of convenient compromise

. . . it is difficult to give any idea of how well she looked in turquoise blue velvet, embroidered in silver fleur de lys with rose brocade bunched up over a white petticoat, and over her head a canopy of pale blue velvet and silver borne by four pages in white satin. Then her jewels were quite lovely – none on her neck, but magnificent ornaments in her hair and on the bodice of her dress. On her powdered hair she wore a tiny turban of turquoise chiffon with a long pink plume coiling round it, and erect at one side two white ostrich tips and a very tall blue aigrette. She had a splendid broad band across the feathers and her curls were caught in a diamond bow.

Lady Warwick's father had died when she was two years old, leaving her an estate in Essex and what was in those days a large income. She grew up to be a beauty and possessed of great charm, and these attributes plus her not inconsiderable fortune soon brought her to the attention of society. Disraeli considered that she would make an ideal wife for Prince Leopold, Queen Victoria's youngest son, and as Daisy made an excellent first impression on the Queen, meetings were arranged between her and the Prince. The outcome of these meetings was, however, that she fell in love with and married the Prince's handsome equerry, Lord Brooke, heir to the Earl of Warwick.

Apart from a streak of waywardness which was passed off then as youthful high spirits, Daisy, with her money, position, charm and beauty, possessed all the requirements for a leader of society and once married she quickly established herself in that role. She loved entertaining and spared no effort or cost to ensure her guests' amusement. A railway station was built near Easton Lodge, her home in Essex, and special trains were always available to guests who wished to go racing, while in the winter horses were provided for anyone who wanted to hunt.

Daisy herself was a fine rider, and during the season hunting took priority over everything. On one occasion in the late 1880s she was summoned to Windsor, much to her chagrin, as she had been planning to hunt the following morning. Since it was a royal command she had no option but to go, and she attended dinner and stayed the night as asked; but the following morning she left on the earliest train dressed in full hunting clothes, apparently deeply shocking the Queen who from her bedroom window had spotted Daisy leaving.

Daisy enhanced her beauty with her taste in clothes, which were the envy of all. Mrs Hwfa Williams wrote about staying with her, 'We all took our best dresses when we went to Easton, but try as we would it was useless to compete with Daisy. Her dresses and tea gowns were always sans pareil, and like all well dressed women she knew how to get the most striking effect from the simplest things.'

Above all, Daisy was possessed of an extraordinarily kind heart, and lavished sympathy and generosity on humans and animals alike. She was genuinely concerned about the plight of the working classes; her employees were well cared for and always looked after in their old age, and no tenant was ever turned out if unable to pay the rent. Daisy with her own funds opened a home for crippled children and started a school of needlework for underprivileged girls in Essex, where beautifully embroidered lingerie was produced and then sold from a shop in Bond Street. This enterprise, despite its excellent cause, received some adverse comment in society, as no lady was supposed to be in trade. Any criticism of her projects was, however, completely ignored by Daisy.

Her love affairs were conducted with the same forthright determination with which she pursued all her interests, and once she had set her sights on someone she let nothing stand in her way. Her first serious liaison was with Lord Charles Beresford, a Royal Navy Commander to whom secret liaisons were nothing new. There is a story about him which demonstrates the pitfalls awaiting unwary lovers. He was staying in a house party at which his mistress was also present. At night when everybody had gone to bed he made his way to her room, let himself in as quietly as possible, and having got undressed climbed into bed. However, it was a big house, the passages were dark, and to his horror he found himself in bed with the Bishop of Oxford and his wife. History does not relate what happened next, but no doubt he was able to make his escape without his identity being revealed.

Lord Charles's love affair with Lady Brooke began in 1886, as a result, according to Lady Augusta Fane, of Daisy accidentally overhearing Lord Charles say that he would never be in love with her – which, as Lady Augusta remarked, 'was a rash thing to say as she soon proved to him'. Daisy's passion for Lord Charles was such that she begged him to throw discretion to the winds and elope with her. Lord Charles was well aware that such an act would mean ruin, not only in society but also to his future in the navy, and towards the end of 1888, when his infatuation had begun to cool, he quietly broke off the affair.

Daisy was distraught by this turn of events, and shortly afterwards, when she discovered that Lady Charles was expecting a baby, she lost all self-control and wrote a hysterical letter to Lord Charles demanding that he leave his wife and return to her. Unfortunately Lord Charles was abroad when the letter arrived, and it was opened by his wife. She immediately gave it to a solicitor, who wrote to Lady Brooke warning her that legal action would be taken if she continued to cause trouble.

At this, Daisy decided to seek help from the Prince of Wales. She was aware of his susceptibilities towards women, and she knew that if she could get him on her side, not only would she be quite safe from Lady Charles's threats, but her somewhat shaky position in society would be firmly re-established. She presented her case to the Prince with all the charm and allure that she could muster, and sure enough the Prince, bowled over by this 'beauty in distress', persuaded the solicitor to show him the letter, and then asked Lady Charles to return it to Daisy. Lady Charles replied that she would do so only on the condition that Daisy stayed out of London for the season. But Daisy, now in a powerful position as mistress to the Prince of Wales, not only refused to meet those terms but prevailed upon the Prince openly to rebuff Lady Charles. At this juncture Lord Charles stepped in to support his wife, and a furious row blew up between him and the Prince of Wales, whom Lord Charles considered was interfering quite unjustly in his affairs.

Lord Charles then went abroad to take command of his ship, and after his departure there was some respite during which Daisy was able to enjoy the full benefits of her position with the Prince. But peace did not last long. Within a year, in September 1890, there had taken place the notorious Tranby Croft affair in which Sir William Gordon-Cumming, an officer in the Guards, was accused of cheating at baccarat while staying at Tranby Croft in a house party which included the Prince of Wales. The host, Arthur Wilson, and the other guests persuaded Gordon-Cumming to sign a paper stating that he would never play cards again. Although he denied the charge Gordon-Cumming was forced to sign to avoid a scandal, whilst his accusers were sworn to secrecy. However, the story soon got around, and Gordon-Cumming brought a libel action against his accusers. The Prince of Wales was called as one of the witnesses. The ensuing scandal seriously threatened both Daisy and the Prince. She was blamed for letting the secret out and became known in a pun on her name as 'the Babbling Brook', while public opinion was extremely hostile towards the Prince.

It was during this delicate time, when further scandal could not be contemplated, that the Beresford affair again raised its head. The Prince had publicly received Lady Brooke, an action which had enraged Lady Charles. She and her friends bombarded her husband with letters until Lord Charles finally wrote to the Prince threatening publicly to call him a blackguard and a coward and to give his reasons for doing so. He sent this letter to his wife, telling her to forward it to the Prince and to inform Lord Salisbury, the Prime Minister, of the whole affair. Here Lady Charles showed unusual caution, for rather than sending the letter straight to the Prince, she sent it with a letter from her to Lord Salisbury. The Prime Minister acted with his accustomed tact and good sense, and managed to persuade Lord Charles not to send the letter to the Prince but to substitute a less provocative missive. Lord Salisbury also promised to act as an intermediary to try to bring the two parties to an agreement, which he had almost managed to do when a highly libellous pamphlet entitled *Lady River*, a thin disguise for Lady Brooke, was published. This enraged the Prince, and when he discovered that its author was Mrs Gerald Paget, Lady Charles's sister, his fury knew no bounds, and he refused to consider coming to an agreement. Lord Charles finally lost patience. He returned to England from his ship, and was on the point of sacrificing his career and exposing the Prince to all the newspapers before fleeing to France with his wife, when Lord Salisbury managed at last to bring the two parties to a settlement. Formal letters of apology were exchanged between the Prince and Lord Charles, and Daisy was temporarily excluded from court. This banishment did not last long, however, and Daisy was soon back at the centre of social activity in London. Despite the letter of apology, the Prince did not really forgive Lord Charles for a long time, and it was many years before he would consent to receive him. Being out of favour with the Prince meant, of course, no invitation to the ball for Lord Charles.

Lord Charles's brother William, who was under no such cloud, did attend, and with his enormous capacity for enjoying himself no doubt derived much pleasure from the occasion.

Lord William Beresford was, like all his family, greatly enamoured of practical jokes, and he loved carrying out daring feats. While he was stationed with his regiment in Cork, a wag bet him that he could not drive his coach down the steep steps of the barracks. The bet was only a joke, as the feat was considered impossible, but the following morning amazed spectators witnessed the sight of a wheel-less coach pulled by four horses and driven by Lord William, coming down the steps and arriving safely at the bottom.

One of his most amusing exploits took place when he was stationed with his regiment in York. A self-opinionated young man had recently joined the regiment, and Lord William considered that he needed taking down a peg or two. So one evening, when the young man had gone out, Lord William and his friends coaxed a donkey up the stairs and into the unfortunate fellow's room, as well as hiding a cock in his dirty laundry basket. When the young man returned, he had a long struggle to remove the donkey, as the poor animal was most unwilling to go back down the stairs. Having finally succeeded and got to bed, the young man was then woken at dawn by the sound of crowing issuing from the clothes basket. Unfortunately it is not known whether Lord William planned any jokes for the Devonshire House Ball and, if so, whether he carried them out.

Lord William spent much of his adult life in India, where initially he was ADC to the Viceroy, Lord Lytton, and afterwards military secretary to the Viceroys Lord Ripon, Lord Dufferin and Lord Lansdowne. Because he was so competent at this job he was persuaded to stay on by each successive Viceroy, but it was active service that Lord William really loved. His conspicuous bravery in the Zulu War earned him a VC and made him a national hero. Judging from the story of how he earned it, his medal was well deserved and his reputation justified. He had led his men in a charge, and had just run his sword through a Zulu chief, when suddenly several thousand Zulus appeared out of the long grass in which they had been completely hidden. Lord William and his men were forced to retreat rapidly, but two men were killed and one was wounded. Although hotly pursued by the enemy, Lord William turned back for the wounded man and somehow managed to lift him on to his horse. They galloped off, assegais flying all around, and twice Lord William was nearly pulled out of the saddle by the wounded soldier who from pain and loss of blood was unable to keep his balance. There was no time to stop and readjust his position, but just as Lord William feared that he could no longer carry the wounded man, a sergeant who had seen the danger rode out and shot Zulu after Zulu as they came within range, allowing Lord William and his burden to reach safety. On hearing that he had been awarded the VC, Lord William agreed to accept it only on condition that the sergeant was also given the award, and as a result both men received the medal.

Lord William returned to England for good in 1894, and in 1895, somewhat to everyone's surprise, he married Lilian, Duchess of Marlborough. She was a twice-widowed American whose first husband had left her a large fortune, a sizeable portion of which had been spent on Blenheim Palace after her second marriage to the Duke of Marlborough. She bore Lord William a son, and they lived happily together until his death in 1900.

At all important dances and receptions it was considered obligatory to invite ambassadors and other leading diplomats. However, since neither they nor their wives were necessarily interesting or entertaining people, they were generally regarded as merely adding to the overcrowding. Indeed, at the Devonshire House Ball the Princess of Wales was said to have been 'horribly bored' by the large number of foreign guests.

There were, of course, notable exceptions, and the Portuguese Ambassador, the Marquis de Soveral, was one. Known as the Blue Monkey because of his blue chin, he has been described as 'nobleman, diplomat, courtier, and ladies' man *par excellence*', and he possessed that unusual combination of brilliance and discretion. He was a close friend of the Prince and Princess of Wales, and had known the Prince ever since their youth when, in Prussia, they had attended 'love orgies' organized by the officers in the Prussian Garde du Corps. The Princess of Wales was

MONS. DE SOVERAL

as Count d'Almada (1640)

especially fond of him, because in her later years when she became increasingly deaf, he was one of the few people with whom she was able to communicate.

At least two of the women at the ball appear to have had liaisons with him. A note from Muriel Wilson, youngest daughter of Arthur Wilson, owner of Tranby Croft, reads : '*Si tu ne viens pas au bal vendredi soir, je ne te parlerai plus jamais, jamais, jamais*. Are you too busy to lunch with me tomorrow (Saturday). I am quite alone but the butler and parrot are excellent chaperones.' Another from Lady de Grey says, 'I am left to my melancholy reflections – when shall I see you again, I wonder.'

It says much for his discretion that he never seemed to provoke husbands. Had he done so, and caused a public scandal, he certainly would not have received an invitation to the Devonshire House Ball.

———————— * ————————

LEFT : *Bertrand de Soveral, the Portuguese Ambassador to the Court of St James, who attended the ball as the seventeenth-century Count d'Almada. At the time of the ball he was conducting two illicit relationships: the first with Muriel Wilson (above), who attended as Vashti; the second with Gladys de Grey. But, unlike Harry Cust, de Soveral was always totally discreet and caused never a ripple on the smooth surface of social convention*

Count Albert Mensdorff, the Austro-Hungarian Ambassador, was another popular diplomat. *Vanity Fair* gives an amusing description of him in its 'Men of the Day' series.

Count Albert Mensdorff is an inveterate bachelor. Sometimes he seems on the point of effecting a matrimonial alliance, but the flutterings of a female heart are never allayed by a proposal. Match-making mothers speak of him with despair. Yet the fact has not prejudiced his position with the sex amongst whom he is vastly admired. He is always to be found at the best houses, in the best clubs and the best set. The King likes him, he is a habitué of Chatsworth.

As well as being a popular figure in society, he was also a most able diplomat. He became an ambassador at the age of forty-two, the youngest man to hold that rank in Europe.

Count Mensdorff went to the ball as Henri III, and, judging from the description of his outfit, took great trouble over his appearance. *Lady's Pictorial* described him thus :

He wore a doublet, trunks and trunk hose of black satin, slashed with little puffs of black silk edged and trimmed with black jet braiding. On the side of the mantilla there was embroidered a broad silver cross of St Esprit. The shoes were black silk with pointed toes, and he carried a silver hilted sword and black velvet scabbard embroidered in gold. On his head he wore a black velvet toque with a white aigrette feather in front, and round his neck he wore a gold jewelled chain and cross of Esprit. On his arms he had long white suede gloves with gilt buttons.

——————— * ———————

Count Albert Mensdorff, the Austro-Hungarian Ambassador. He took the greatest care over his costume as Henry III of France, wearing the broad silver cross of St Esprit and repeating the motif on his cloak

The Hon. Mrs George Curzon as Valentina Visconti of Milan.
Born Mary Leiter of Chicago, the daughter of a founder of the Marshall
Field department store, she was brought to Europe on the grand tour by her
mother. When she met George Curzon in London in 1890 she promptly
fell in love with him and they were married in Washington
five years later

There were a number of Americans at the ball, some of whom were married to Englishmen. Some of these unions, such as that of Lord and Lady Randolph Churchill and Mr and Mrs Curzon, were love matches, but many were arranged with a view, on the American side, of increasing social status, and on the English side of cornering a large dowry. The Duchess of Marlborough was a victim of this practice. Consuelo

———————— * ————————

Consuelo, Duchess of Marlborough, despite being seven months pregnant,
attended the ball in the tightly laced costume of the wife of the French
ambassador at the court of Catherine the Great. Born Consuelo
Vanderbilt, she had been forced to marry the 9th Duke of Marlborough by
her ambitious mother, despite the fact that she was very much in love with
another man. Although her Vanderbilt inheritance was invaluable to the
Marlboroughs, the marriage was to prove disastrously unhappy

THE DUCHESS OF MARLBOROUGH
as the wife of the French Ambassador at the
Court of Catherine of Russia

[111]

Vanderbilt, with her heart-shaped face and long elegant neck, was not only beautiful, she was also intelligent. But her main asset in her future husband's eyes was her fortune. The Marlboroughs were in need of funds for the maintenance of Blenheim, their vast palace near Oxford, and marrying an heiress was the only way to procure immediately the sum required. Consuelo, in love with another man, did all she could to refuse, but her mother, seeing the marriage as a social advancement to herself, thwarted all her daughter's attempts to avoid the union. Plans to elope were intercepted, and Consuelo was locked in her room for four days prior to the wedding. On the day, her veil had to be extra thick, so ravaged was her face from crying.

The wedding was in 1895, and when the ball took place Consuelo was seven months pregnant. However, her figure was extremely well disguised by her eighteenth-century French costume, a dress of palest green satin, richly embroidered. Her hair was hooped and powdered, and her dress was decorated with garlands of roses, set off with many jewels including a superb diamond girdle.

The *New York World*, which claimed to have been given a description of the ball by one of the guests, said that although she looked magnificent, 'she did not go into supper with the royalties and played a comparatively unimportant part in the ball,' though it was hardly surprising considering her condition.

Another American who was unhappily married to an English duke was the Duchess of Devonshire's daughter-in-law from her first marriage to the Duke of Manchester. Also called Consuelo, she was one of four children of Mr and Mrs Yznaga from Louisiana. They were not enormously rich, having suffered reverses of fortune after the Civil War, and unlike the young Duchess of Marlborough, Consuelo Yznaga was happy with her engagement, the result of the Duke of Manchester (then Lord Mandeville) contracting typhoid fever while staying with the Yznagas and having to remain with them for a slow convalescence, during which time he and Consuelo fell in love. The Duke and Duchess of Manchester were far from happy at the engagement, and the Duke was said to be nearly heartbroken at the idea of his son marrying a 'little American savage'. However, they gave their consent after they met her, as she made an excellent impression with her beauty, charm and warm-heartedness.

The couple were married in 1876, but the marriage did not prove happy. The Duke deserted Consuelo for a time for a music-hall singer called Bessy Bellwood, and it was during this liaison that he was called as a police witness after Miss Bellwood had assaulted a cab driver who was trying to collect his fare. According to a contemporary account, 'Everybody's attention was directed to his disgraceful position. Many similar and no less shameful incidents occurred . . .' In 1889 the Duke was declared bankrupt, and in 1890 he died – no doubt to his wife's relief, though her life became no happier as a result, for her twin daughters died young and her son proved to be as immoral as his father.

Consuelo was much loved by all who knew her, although she was quite eccentric, particularly in her dress. There is an account of her before she married going to a party where, on arrival, she discarded her cloak to reveal 'a dress that could only be described as a voluminous thing like a balloon, a sort of Mother Hubbard gown, or a big white nightgown'. This was during the days of tight fitting waists and bodices, and her dress caused great embarrassment to her young escort, who had much difficulty in persuading her to tie a ribbon round her waist. On another occasion after she was widowed she was on her way to a ball, when she suddenly turned to her young female companion and said 'My stays are so tight, hot and boring' and immediately proceeded to remove them.

So Consuelo must have loved the opportunity to give her imagination full rein when planning a costume for the ball. She went as Anne of Austria, in a very striking gown of white and silver satin, decorated with swags of gold satin. On her head she wore a diamond crown with a large single pearl ornament in the centre of her forehead.

Both her sisters were at the ball: Natica, who was married to Sir John Lister Kaye, went as the Duchesse de Guise; and Emily, who was a great favourite in English society and taught Edward VII to play the banjo. Emily went as Cydalise of the Comédie Italienne, from the time of Louis XV, dressed in a blue satin dress embroidered with gold and silver thread.

So many rich young heiresses were brought from the States to Europe in the last years of the nineteenth century that they were referred to as the American Invasion, and several of them were to marry into English society. The three Yznaga sisters from Louisiana were a case in point. Consuelo married the 8th Duke of Manchester and was thus Duchess Louisa's daughter-in-law. Her sister Emilia (left) attended the ball as Cydalise of the Comedie Italienne during the reign of Louis XV, while her third sister, Natica (left) attended the ball as Cydalise of the Comedie Italienne during the reign of Louis XV, while her third sister, Natica (right), married to Sir John Lister Kaye, chose to represent the Duchess of Guise of the reign of Henry III of France

The young Duke of Manchester, Consuelo's son, inherited little in the way of money from his father and did nothing himself to rectify the situation, being dissipated, spendthrift and a thoroughly bad hat. Not only did his bills remain unpaid, but the housekeeper at his Huntingdonshire home, Kimbolton, whose wages had not been paid, felt obliged to buy tinned food and whisky out of her own savings so that there would be something to offer the Duke's friends when he invited them to stay.

*May Goelet, a young heiress from New York, was the object of the
attention of the 9th Duke of Manchester, Consuelo's son, but luckily she
was able to resist his doubtful charms. May attended the Devonshire House
Ball as Scherazade, in a Parisian costume of multi-coloured gauze heavily
embroidered with precious stones*

He was determined to find himself an heiress (which he eventually did, though he got hold of her money in a most underhand way) and in 1897 he was enthusiastically paying court to May Goelet from New York. Her mother had been a Miss Wilson, one of a family noted for their ambitious marriages, and now Mrs Goelet had brought her daughter to Europe in the hope of finding an eligible young nobleman for her. A duke, provided he was half-way respectable, would have been ideal, but even the Goelets drew the line at the Duke of Manchester. The young duke tried to force their hand by announcing his engagement to Miss Goelet in the paper, but her father, having said that he would rather see his daughter dead than married to the Duke of Manchester, had the announcement withdrawn. However, they were determined not to let such an incident ruin their social life, and an invitation to the Devonshire House Ball was an assurance to the family that they were accepted, indeed well ensconced, in English society. A newspaper account describes them at the ball:

High on the list in gorgeousness of attire was another American lady, Mrs Ogden Goelet. Her dress was black with a long black train, and marvellously ornamented with white and black pearls. She has made a success where she was unheard of last winter. The Queen herself when she went to Cimiez went on the Prince's yacht where the Goelets were staying.

Miss Goelet, who is the greatest success of the season in the American contingent, represented Sheherezade in an Eastern dress of gold gauze, having three separate gauze sashes in pink, mauve and blue. The embroidery on the dress was done in different coloured precious stones and made in Paris. The headdress was a helmet with side pieces over each ear, on one side a scarlet flower, and on the other a white lotus lily.

There are many references in contemporary accounts to the smartness and chic of the American women in English society, and one of those most frequently mentioned was Mrs Arthur Paget. Born Minnie Stevens, she was the daughter of Mr Paran Stevens of Boston, who had built up a fortune in hotels which, according to an acquaintance, 'he collected as assiduously as Commodore Vanderbilt collects railroads'.

Minnie was brought up in New York, and her mother was so ambitious for her that on one occasion, when there were two fashionable opening

Minnie Stevens of Boston caused quite a stir when she arrived in England in the 1870s. Her final choice of husband was a guards officer, Arthur Paget, whom she married in 1878. Like Lady de Grey, she chose to go to the Devonshire House Ball as Cleopatra, but her costume was very different (see page 85). Minnie went to Worth, who produced a dress of white and gold, covered in jewels, producing a stunning effect. Sadly, this magnificent costume was to fetch a mere £9 after Minnie's death

Minnie's husband, Colonel Arthur Paget as Edward, the Black Prince. The victor of Crécy and Poitiers presumably was an apt choice for a regular soldier, but his chain mail must have been remarkably uncomfortable on a hot summer's evening

nights on the same evening, Mrs Stevens insisted that her daughter should leave one at the interval and go to the other, in order that she would be seen at both. After her father's death in 1872, Minnie spent much time in England, and quickly became a favourite at Marlborough House, for the Prince of Wales had always taken kindly to Americans.

Not everyone, however, thought so favourably of Minnie. Frances, Countess of Waldegrave described her as 'an awful story teller, who never indulges in a word of truth, even to her most intimate friends'. The Duchess of Marlborough wrote about a visit she paid in the 1890s to the then Mrs Arthur Paget : ' . . .she was considered handsome; to me, with her quick wit and worldly standards, she was Becky Sharp incarnate. She received us with a mixture of the affection due to an old friend, and the condescension that seemed to infect the habitués of the inner circles of London society. I realized with a surge of acute discomfort that I was being appraised by a pair of hard green eyes.'

Minnie was twenty-five when, in 1878, after considering several eligible suitors, she finally married Arthur Paget, a handsome and rich officer in the Brigade of Guards. From then on she threw herself enthusiastically into enjoying life as a fashionable socialite, and was described in one paper as 'one of the most brilliant leaders of society, daring in her entertainment and original in her dress'.

Her costume for the ball, was made by Worth in Paris, and took weeks of planning and making. As Cleopatra, she must have been slightly disappointed to find two other Cleopatras, one of whom was Lady de Grey. The descriptions of her in the press were, perhaps, some consolation. The *New York World* described her outfit as

. . . a marvellous story in white and gold, and . . . literally covered in jewels. Nothing like such gems on the American lady's dress were ever seen in London or elsewhere. The costume was simply ablaze with diamonds, rubies and emeralds. When she entered, people accustomed to the greatest displays of jewels the world has ever known, gasped with wonder and astonishment. Lady de Grey's dress, although it cost $6000, was quite eclipsed by Mrs Paget's costume.

The *Daily Mail* was also lavish in its praise for her: '. . . small, lithe, and seductive, a lovely serpent of the old Nile, Mrs Arthur Paget seemed born to play the part of Cleopatra in such a pageant for she is dark haired, with a low white brow, and scarlet lips, and her beautiful big eyes are like star sapphires so mysteriously, darkly blue are they.'

After she died in 1911 her clothes were sold by auction. All her beautiful dresses went for very little, and her Cleopatra costume fetched only £9. One newspaper account ends its description of the sale with the sad comment, 'the frocks which once graced a society leader will soon perhaps be found in the second hand clothes shops of Bayswater and Whitechapel'.

Perhaps the most famous American woman living in England to attend the ball was Lady Randolph Churchill. Always original in her dress, her costume for the ball was a masterpiece. She represented Empress Theodora in a dress which came from a design by Benjamin Constant and was made by Worth. It was of mauve satin embroidered with gold, diamonds and colours, the border of the *étole* being beautifully embroidered in coloured angels' heads. The sleeves were of violet mousseline studded with silver paillettes, and on her head she wore a Byzantine head-dress decorated with emeralds and diamonds. The effect was such that one newspaper described her as being 'beautifully attired as Empress Theodora, her costume being one of the most striking to be seen at the ball'. Another report, however, describes one pear-shaped emerald falling right on to her nose, producing 'rather a funny effect'.

Jennie was born in Brooklyn in 1854, the second of three daughters of Mr Leonard Jerome. Her father was a wildly extravagant man who twice faced financial ruin, but each time he managed to remake his fortune, and Jennie and her sisters, Clara and Leonie, spent a very happy childhood in New York. In 1870, when Jennie was sixteen, her mother and two sisters sailed for Europe where her elder sister Clara was to be presented to Napoleon III and the Empress Eugénie. Much to Jennie's disappointment she missed making her début in Paris, as the Franco-Prussian War began, and the Jeromes were forced to flee. They were very lucky to get away; they caught what proved to be the last train out of Paris, carrying what they could tied up in tablecloths. Their maid, who returned home planning to pack their trunks and follow the next day, was forced by the Prussians to remain in Paris throughout the siege.

The family, joined by Leonard, rented a house in the Isle of Wight, and it was here that Jennie met, and after a whirlwind three-day romance, became engaged to Lord Randolph Churchill. To begin with, there was parental opposition on both sides, but the young couple steadfastly refused to be swayed, and on 15 April 1874 they were married in New York.

At the outset of their married life Lord and Lady Randolph seemed to have everything going for them. She was lovely, with dark brown hair, dark, panther-like eyes and striking features that owed some of their beauty to the Red Indian blood inherited from her mother. She had an

LADY RANDOLPH CHURCHILL

as the Empress Theodora, wife of Justinian

[120]

enthusiasm, generosity and warmth that endeared her to all who met her. Lord Randolph was already making a name for himself in politics, and his intelligence and quick wit, plus her beauty and charm helped to make them one of the most popular young couples in London.

However, by the time of the Devonshire House Ball Lord Randolph was dead and poor Jennie had endured much suffering and tragedy. The first blow occurred in 1876 when, because of the part played by Lord Randolph in supporting his brother Lord Blandford in the Aylesford case, the Prince of Wales announced that he would enter no house in England that opened its doors to the Churchills. So, rather than stay in England to be snubbed and ignored by people whom they had thought to be friends, Lord and Lady Randolph moved to Ireland, where Lord Randolph acted as unofficial secretary to his father, who was Lord Lieutenant there.

The quarrel with the Prince of Wales was finally made up in 1883, and at the election of 1885 Lord Randolph accepted the office of Secretary of State for India, which was one of the most important posts in the government. In 1886, when Lord Salisbury became Prime Minister, Lord Randolph was appointed Leader of the House of Commons and Chancellor of the Exchequer. Jennie, who was extremely ambitious for her husband, took it for granted that he would one day be Prime Minister. But, just as he seemed set to conquer the political world, he disagreed with the Cabinet over the allocation of finance to the armed services and handed in his resignation. He gambled on this, thinking that either this move would bring down the government and he would be made Prime Minister, or he would be begged to stay and given increased power. His bluff was called, however, and Lord Salisbury accepted his resignation.

---
*

Lady Randolph Churchill as Theodora, consort of the Byzantine Emperor, Justinian. Her very rich dress, reflecting Byzantine themes in the embroidered 'étole' and the headdress, was designed for her by Benjamin Constant and made by Worth. Jennie must have viewed the Devonshire House Ball with mixed feelings, for it was the first time she had seen her lover, Count Kinsky, since his marriage, but it was also the evening that she first set eyes on her future husband, George Cornwallis West

Lord Randolph had not mentioned the matter to his family, and the first Jennie knew of it was when she read the announcement in the paper the following morning. This marked the end of Lord Randolph's career, and it was from this time on that the syphilis which eventually killed him began its slow, insidious eating away of his mind and body.

These must have been nightmare days for Jennie, for not only was she bitterly disappointed at the sudden halt in her husband's career, but she also had to watch helplessly while his health deteriorated. More and more she turned for support to an Austrian diplomatic attaché, Count Charles Kinsky. He was witty and charming, a good dancer and a brilliant rider, having won the Grand National on his own mare, Zoedone, in 1883. He returned Jennie's affections, and they came to rely on each other heavily. His parents knew about this love affair, although at first they were not unduly worried for they knew that there would be no question of Lady Randolph divorcing her husband. However, when Lord Randolph's illness became generally known, they did become concerned. First, Lady Randolph had no heraldic quarterings (most important to Austrians of aristocratic family), nor was she a Catholic. Secondly, at forty-one she was unlikely to produce an heir. In 1894, under great pressure from his parents, who threatened to cut off all financial support if he married Jennie, Charles Kinsky became engaged to a young Austrian countess. Much as he adored Jennie, he desperately needed his parents' financial aid in order to support his extravagant living.

Jennie received the news by telegram, while enduring a tortuous tour of the East with her husband who was now very near his end. She wrote to her sister Leonie begging her to try to stop the marriage, but although Leonie did her best, her efforts were to no avail, and on 9 January 1895 Kinsky married the countess. Two weeks later, after a long and terrible illness which caused great suffering not only to him but to all his family, Lord Randolph Churchill died.

Two years later, Kinsky, his wife and Jennie attended the Devonshire House Ball, and it was here that Jennie first set eyes on her future husband, George Cornwallis West, who was part of the entourage of his sister, the Princess of Pless. But at this time Jennie was alone, and despite her popularity and being surrounded by friends, it seems that she must

Count Charles Kinsky, the Austrian diplomatic attaché who stole Jennie
Churchill's heart. A brilliant rider, he had won the Grand National on
his mare Zoedone in 1883, when this drawing was made of him

have suffered at the ball, seeing Kinsky with his wife and knowing that he was now unobtainable. In Victorian society 'appearances' were all important, however, and if an illicit liaison were going on no hint of it whatsoever was permitted to be given by the lovers in public. The same applied when such a liaison ended, and however unhappy or jealous an overthrown partner might feel, he or she had to display a brave face and the proverbial stiff upper lip.

Possibly the most ingenious costume at the ball was worn by a most remarkable American woman. This was a Mrs Ronalds, a trained singer from New York who came to Europe after the failure of her marriage. Her beauty and her fine voice soon attracted attention in Paris, and she became one of the Empress Eugénie's circle at the Tuileries. After the fall of the French Empire in 1870 she moved to London, where she was accepted as one of the most talented women in society. She was a close friend and mentor of Sir Arthur Sullivan, and the first phonographic record ever made of 'The Lost Chord' was sung by Mrs Ronalds. Sir Arthur had written it as a posthumous tribute to his brother, and after Mrs Ronalds died the manuscript was, on her instructions, buried with her.

She went to the ball as Euterpe, 'The Spirit of Music', in a yellow satin gown embroidered with bars from Verdi's *Ballo in Maschera*, and a cloak of white and green satin embroidered with musical instruments. On her head she wore a crown in the shape of a diamond lyre surrounded by sparkling crochets and quavers, which was lit by electricity by means of a tiny battery hidden in her hair.

She had worn exactly the same outfit at a fancy dress ball given by her father in New York thirty years before, except on that occasion the head-dress was lit by tiny gas jets which were supplied by a holder hidden in her hair.

Mrs Ronalds as Euterpe, the Spirit of Music. A trained singer from New York, she became a close friend of the composer, Sir Arthur Sullivan. Her gown of yellow satin was embroidered with bars from Verdi's opera, 'Ballo in Maschera', while her ingenious headdress consisted of a crown surmounted by a diamond lyre, surrounded by crochets and quavers that could be lit up by electricity from a tiny battery hidden in her hair

THE steady stream of guests continued up the stairs and, having made their greeting, passed on into the ballroom. This, like all the reception rooms, was amassed with flowers : orchids, lilies and many other exotic plants from the great conservatory at Chatsworth were banked up around the room to glorious effect, further enhanced by the reflection from the great mirrors between the windows. Footmen in eighteenth-century livery handed round champagne, while the guests greeted one another and gazed at a scene with which even those well accustomed to grandeur and splendour could not fail to be impressed.

At quarter past eleven, a loud cheer from the crowd outside hailed the arrival of the royal party. The supreme irony was that although the Devonshire House Ball was held to honour Queen Victoria's Diamond Jubilee and the sixty years of her reign, the Queen was too frail to be able to attend. After the death of the Prince Consort in 1861, Victoria had retired into long, sad years of seclusion, ignoring the fulminations of *The Times*, the threats of the republicans and the murmurs of disapproval from the general public. But, with the 1880s, her return to the public stage had brought her immense popularity : she had become a cherished institution. The acclamation reached its climax with the celebration of her Golden Jubilee in 1887, when she was able to participate with immense gusto, attending parties at Buckingham Palace and a thanksgiving service at Westminster Abbey on the anniversary of her accession, 20 June 1837. She herself described this in her journal, 'this never-to-be-forgotten day will always leave the most gratifying and heart-stirring memories behind'.

But, ten years later, sorrow and age had sapped her energies. Guests were received by her in her wheel chair, while the day of processions and thanksgiving, 22 June, was confined to a short service *outside* St Paul's Cathedral, with the Queen in her open laundau. The major role of attending receptions, parties and celebrations, and of greeting all the representatives of Empire that poured into London, fell upon the shoulders of the Queen's eldest son, Albert Edward, Prince of Wales. With his wife, the Danish Princess Alexandra by his side, he had become the focus of all social activities. During the week before the Devonshire House Ball, he had been desperately busy attending daily functions and engagements concerning the Jubilee. A private ball, with all his friends around him, must have come as a welcome break from his official duties.

A flutter of excitement ran through the guests as the band struck up the National Anthem. The Duke and Duchess stood ready to greet the royal party, while the guests still downstairs stood aside, bowing and curtseying as the Prince and Princess, accompanied by members of their family, slowly made their way up the circular staircase. The Princess of Wales, as Marguerite de Valois, looked magnificent in a dress of white satin embroidered in gold with a long train of gold cloth borne by two pages. Her stomacher was ablaze with precious stones, her neck encircled with row upon row of pearls, and a diamond crown adorned on her head. With her were her three daughters, Princess Louise, Duchess of Fife, Princess Maud, wife of Prince Charles of Denmark, who became King Haakon VII of Norway, and Princess Victoria. The Prince of Wales represented the Grand Master of the Knights Hospitallers of St John of Jerusalem and Chevalier of Malta. Stout but dignified, he looked most picturesque in his Elizabethan dress of a doublet of black velvet embroidered in steel and jet, with trunks of grey silk slashed with black velvet straps wrought with steel. He wore a high hat trimmed with white plumes, and high black turreted boots with large silver spurs. On his doublet he had a diamond Maltese cross, with the genuine Order of St John of Jerusalem of Malta.

-----------------------------------* -----------------------------------

Although the Devonshire House Ball was held to celebrate the Diamond Jubilee of Queen Victoria, she was too frail to attend. Thus the guests of honour were the Prince and Princess of Wales and their family and attendants. The Prince chose to represent the Grand Master of the Knights Hospitallers of St John of Jerusalem and Chevalier of Malta

HRH THE PRINCE OF WALES
as Grand Prior of the Order of St John of Jerusalem

The Princess of Wales elected to represent Marguerite de Valois, daughter of Henry II of France and Catherine de' Medici, who married her cousin, Henry of Navarre, in 1572. Around her neck she wore a collar of pearls – a style that she made fashionable in England – while more rows of pearls fell to her waist

Lady Alington represented the Duchess of Nevers, a lady of Marguerite's court

George, Duke of York, son of the Prince and Princess of Wales, broke away from the Valois theme to represent George Clifford, Earl of Cumberland during the reign of Elizabeth I and her Master of the Tilts. His Duchess, May of Teck, attended the ball as a lady of her mother-in-law's French court in a dress of vivid sky-blue satin wrought with silver

Accompanying the Princess of Wales as ladies of Marguerite's court were two of her daughters, Victoria (seated centre) and Maud (seated left) who was married to Prince Charles of Denmark (left)

LEFT : *Princess Mary, Duchess of Teck, in a tribute to her ancestress, Electress Sophia of Hanover.*
Mary was one of the royal children born as a result of the 'Matrimonial Race' following the death of the Prince
Regent's daughter in 1817. The winner of the race turned out to be Victoria, daughter of George III's fourth son,
but the tenth son, Adolphus, Duke of Cambridge, duly produced three children, including Mary. As she grew up,
she became enormously fat, and this seemed to make her a difficult marriage proposition. But the problem was
overcome when a handsome young Austrian officer, Prince Francis of Teck (right), was persuaded to offer his hand.
His one great ambition was to become a Royal Highness, but sadly even marriage to 'Fat Mary' did not achieve
this, and his disappointment drove him finally to mental breakdown. He attended the ball as a
captain of the eighteenth-century French royal guard

Having received the Prince and Princess and their entourage, the Duke and Duchess led them across the ballroom to the Saloon. The guests lined the path, bowing and curtseying in a brilliant kaleidoscope of colours and glittering jewels as the Prince greeted his friends right and left, beaming broadly.

The Prince and Princess took their places at the centre of the dais from where they were to watch the processions, with the rest of the royal party grouped behind them. The Prince's daughter-in-law the Duchess of York, later to become Queen Mary, was dressed as a lady of the court of Marguerite de Valois in vivid sky-blue satin wrought with silver, her hair threaded with silver and diamond ornaments. Princess Charles of Denmark, also as a lady of the court, looked lovely in palest pink satin embroidered with pink and silver. The Duke and Duchess of Fife represented a lady and gentleman from the court of Henri II. To the left of Princess of Wales sat Mary, Duchess of Teck, granddaughter of George III and the mother of the Duchess of York. She was an elderly woman now, and vastly overweight, but her gaiety and enthusiasm for life was undaunted and she watched the spectacle before her with interest and amusement. She made an imposing figure as her ancestress, the Electress Sophia of Hanover, mother of George I, in a gorgeous dress of orange velvet trimmed with ermine.

Princess Victoria, another lady of the court of Marguerite de Valois, was also enjoying herself. She had led a somewhat unhappy life, kept at home by her mother as a companion and lady-in-waiting and never allowed to marry. So an evening of entertainment, such as the Devonshire House Ball, must have been a welcome diversion from the restricted and sheltered life she normally led.

While the Royal Family took their places, the other guests were organizing themselves into their courts and processions, which had been carefully planned and rehearsed beforehand. Those who were not part of any procession lined the room and crowded the doorways, all agog for what promised to be a brilliant display.

Will Somers, in reality Henry VIII's court jester rather than Elizabeth I's, was played by Henry Holden

*

The Elizabethan Court at the ball was led by Lady Tweedmouth as Elizabeth I, with her husband as the Queen's great favourite, Robert Dudley, Earl of Leicester

LADY TWEEDMOUTH
as Queen Elizabeth
LORD TWEEDMOUTH
as the Earl of Leicester

[131]

The first procession to enter the Saloon was the English Court. This was led by Queen Elizabeth I, played by Lady Tweedmouth, who was almost unrecognizable, so convincing was her costume and hairstyle. She wore a full hooped skirt of rich brocade in old gold and white, with a huge collar and stiff turned-back cuffs of old lace and gold. Pearls were worn over the front of the bodice, and arranged in profusion in her coiffure. One newspaper remarked that 'so realistic was she that she might have stepped out of her frame at the National Portrait Gallery'. Accompanying the Queen was a guard of six yeomen, whose costumes had been copied exactly from Holbein's painting of the Field of the Cloth of Gold at Hampton Court. Four yeomen, one of whom was the Duke of Roxburgh, carried a white and gold canopy over the Queen, who was followed by her Court Jester, Will Somers, played by Henry Holden, who was greeted by a hearty guffaw from the Prince of Wales.

Practically every well-known Elizabethan figure was represented. Lady Tweedmouth's husband impersonated Robert Dudley, the Earl of Leicester, and the Earl of Essex represented Robert Devereux, the Earl of Elizabethan days. Behind these was Lord Darnley, carrying the sword of state, Sir Philip Sydney, Sir Walter Raleigh and Sir Francis Drake. Then came the Archbishop of Canterbury, Thomas Cranmer, played by the philanthropist Lord Rowton, who was magnificently attired in gold and white robes and a mitre.

Queen Elizabeth's rival, Mary Queen of Scots, formed part of this procession. She was represented by Lady Edmonstone in a white satin robe with long hanging sleeves of velvet and a pearl Mary Stuart cap with a long *lisse* veil. She was accompanied by a large entourage, with Lady de Ramsay, Lord Herbert of Cherbury and Lord James Murray among the characters represented.

Lord Darnley was represented by John Leslie,
husband of Jennie Churchill's sister, Leonie

Among Elizabeth I's courtiers was the Duchess of
Roxburghe representing the formidable Bess of
Hardwick, founder of the Cavendish family fortunes
and builder of the first Chatsworth

THE MARCHIONESS OF LANSDOWNE
*as Lady Keith, wife to the British Ambassador at
the Court of Maria Theresa*

The Elizabethan Court was followed by the Austrian Court of Maria Theresa, with Lady Londonderry as a suitably glorious and regal Empress. She was accompanied by the Marchioness of Lansdowne as Lady Keith, the friend of the Empress, and the Marquis of Lansdowne as Prince Kaunitz, Chamberlain to Her Majesty. Five archdukes and archduchesses, all in white and silver with powdered hair, attended her, followed by various Austrian princes and princesses, and a Coldstreamer in Vienna, played by Lord Winchester. Led by Lady Londonderry, the members of the court walked one by one to the foot of the dais, and curtseyed or bowed to the royal party before passing on into the ballroom.

———————— * ————————

The Austrian procession was led by Lady Londonderry (page 80) as Maria Theresa, Empress of Austria, and her consort Emperor Francis I was represented by the Marchioness's son, Viscount Castlereagh (left). The Marchioness of Lansdowne (right) took part in this procession as Lady Keith, wife of the British Ambassador to Vienna

Next to be received was the Russian court of the Empress Catherine the Great. The Empress was represented by Lady Raincliffe, who, tall and fair, made a stately figure in her white satin dress embroidered with gold and decorated with rubies. Attached to her dress was an ermine-lined yellow velvet train with the Russian Imperial double-headed eagle embroidered in black. Lord Henry Bentinck as Prince Poniatowski, later King of Poland, walked before the Empress, attired in green and gold with white vest and breeches and the blue ribbon of an order around his neck. They were followed by Prince Pless as Prince Orloff, and an Imperial Guard of seven men in fine white uniforms with light blue facings and gold lacing. Attending the Empress was a suite of ladies, including the Duchess of Marlborough. There were also gentlemen of the court, including the Duke of Marlborough in his expensive and extravagant outfit. Two trumpeters and three negro attendants in yellow and crimson brought up the rear of this procession, which had particularly pleased the Princess of Wales, who, whilst receiving, had frequently turned to the Prince to make some appreciative remark.

Empress Catherine and her retinue were followed by the Orientals. This was headed by the Duchess of Devonshire herself, who was carried into the Saloon on a palanquin by slaves holding huge fans. Carrying this was quite a strain for its bearers; the Duchess was no light weight, and the canopy was made of wood, so it was with some relief that the slaves set the palanquin down for the Duchess to alight.

———————— * ————————

Lady Raincliffe as Catherine II, Empress of All the Russias. As this photograph shows, the Viscountess cut a splendid figure in her white satin dress with red and gold decoration, and her yellow velvet train embroidered with the Imperial eagle

[136]

VISCOUNTESS RAINCLIFFE
as Catherine II of Russia

Daisy, Princess of Pless as the Queen of Sheba in a dress of purple gauze shot with
gold and decorated with jewels. Among her retinue was her brother, George
Cornwallis West, OPPOSITE PAGE, *blacked up as a slave and dressed, in his*
words, 'in garments like multi-coloured bed quilts'. His disguise may have
thwarted his love life, but it was at the Devonshire House Ball that he first met his
future wife, Jennie Churchill

She was followed by several Egyptian kings and queens, which was a
popular disguise for there were several representing the same character.
There were two Queens of Sheba, for example: Lady Cynthia Graham
and Daisy, Princess of Pless. It was unfortunate for Lady Cynthia that her
rival should be the Princess of Pless, as although the former's attire was
lovely, she did not have the resources with which to compete with the
princess, whose garment and jewels were quite superb. Her dress was of
purple gauze shot with gold and embroidered with turquoise, silver and
gold, and every sort of precious and semi-precious stones. She was
preceded by two tall, pretty girls as Amazonian guards, and behind her
were five little Ethiopian boys carrying her train. A number of slaves
completed her entourage, including her brother, George Cornwallis

West. As a young cadet in the army he had been unable to afford an outfit so, with the bribe of a free costume, his sister had enlisted him to join her retinue. George, however, was most dissatisfied with his dress, and could not understand why 'the Queen of Sheba's male attendants were full-blooded negroes and dressed in garments like multi-coloured bed quilts'. He hated having to blacken his face, as none of his girlfriends recognized or appreciated him in such disguise. He was one of the few people who appeared to gain no enjoyment from the ball, and he left early feeling very resentful towards the theatrical designer who was responsible for his costume. Perhaps he would have been less disgruntled had he known that Lady Randolph Churchill, whom he met for the first time that evening, was later to become his wife.

MRS ASQUITH

as an Oriental Snake Charmer

There were many well-known beauties in the Oriental procession, including Lady de Grey, Lady Dudley, Lady Randolph Churchill and Miss Muriel Wilson, the daughter of Arthur Wilson. Miss Wilson – casting longing glances in de Soveral's direction – was dressed as Vashti, with a band of diamonds on her head from which rose a diamond quill on one side and a pomegranate bloom on the other. Margot Asquith was typically original in her choice of outfit as an Oriental snake-charmer, with papier mâché snakes wound round the bodice of her sequinned dress, and on her head a sequinned snake rising from her curls.

As the members of this procession passed in front of the Royal Family, they salaamed in Eastern fashion, which caused much amusement.

---------------- * ----------------

Margot Asquith as an Oriental snake charmer, complete with papier mâché snakes. Margot, one of the large and eccentric family of Sir Charles Tennant, was an ebullient and fascinating character, though no great beauty – she once said, 'I have no face, only two profiles'. In 1894 she married the rising Liberal politician, Henry Asquith, who attended the Devonshire House Ball as a Roundhead soldier, but unfortunately did not pose for a photograph

Next to make their appearance was the Italian group. Poor Mrs Hwfa Williams, in her spy hole upstairs, must have found this procession very tantalizing after all the hard work she had put into organizing it. There were Italian characters from every century, and from all over the country. Lady Mar and Kellie made an exceptionally beautiful Beatrice, her hair falling in long tresses from under a small green velvet cap and gold crown with a long veil of *mousseline de soie*. Lord and Lady Stavordale represented Petrarch and Laura, and Lord Hyde dressed as Romeo, though unaccompanied by a Juliet. Lord Peel was a doge of Venice, and there were several ladies from Venice, Florence and Verona, each with the escutcheon of their town embroidered on their dresses. The Duke and Duchess of Portland made a splendid Duce and Duchessa di Sauvio, he in black velvet embroidered in jet, and she in a white and silver dress with a silver Venetian collar and a train of silver brocade wrought with pearls and lined in pale blue silk. But although they made a lovely picture, the Duke's disguise was nearly the cause of a disaster. He described the incident thus in his book, *Men, Women and Things*: 'I wore rather a light coloured wig, and my moustache was enlarged with yellow cotton wool to match the wig. After supper I committed the terrible anachronism of lighting a cigarette; and I was promptly repaid for my sin by my moustache catching fire. I therefore snatched it off, amid the jeers of my friends, and threw it into a finger glass.' Added to this, the Duchess found the weight of her wig a great strain, which made them decide that at future fancy dress entertainments they would remain in their ordinary clothes.

The members of this group had been rehearsing twice a week for the past month, and they were much applauded for the stylish execution of their procession and the quadrille that they performed afterwards.

———————————— * ————————————

The Italian procession had been very carefully prepared for the ball, with its participants going twice weekly to rehearsals for their quadrilles. Members of the procession included several members of the Souls (see page 76), and the beautiful young Countess of Mar and Kellie as Dante's Beatrice

THE COUNTESS OF MAR & KELLIE

as Dante's Beatrice

ABOVE LEFT : *Lord Stavordale as Petrarch;*
ABOVE RIGHT : *Lady Robert Cecil as*
Valentine Visconti; and BELOW : *young*
Master Evelyn de Rothschild as page to the
Dogaressa of Venice

LEFT : *Lady Algernon Gordon Lennox went to the ball as the Princesse de Lamballe,*
Marie Antoinette's ill-fated friend whose severed head was used as a football after she was
guillotined in the Revolution. RIGHT : *Lady Isobel Stanley, daughter of the 16th Earl of*
Derby, in hunting costume from the reign of Louis XVI

The Italians were followed by those in costumes from the reigns of
Louis XV and Louis XVI. There were some spectacular and extravagant
creations in these courts, led by Lady Warwick as Marie Antoinette. Lady
Algernon Gordon Lennox, who went as Princesse de Lamballe, wore a
dress with such enormous panniers that she had to go sideways through
the wide doors of Devonshire House. Mrs Keppel made a beautiful
Madame de Polignac; the panniers she wore were part of a genuine dress
of the period, all over the satin-embroidered dress were silk flowers, while
around her neck and pinned to her bodice were diamonds which had been
reset into the style of the time. There were Watteau shepherdesses and
paysannes galantes in ankle-length dresses carrying crooks wreathed with
flowers. Lady Isobel Stanley looked most striking in a Louis XVI
hunting costume. Even the Three Musketeers were not forgotten, with
William James representing d'Artagnan. But despite the beauty and
lavishness of most of the outfits of this period, it was the Duchess of
Sutherland in her simple costume as Charlotte Corday who stood out
above all the others.

[145]

LADY GERARD

as Astarte, Goddess of the Moon

The last procession to make an appearance was that of the 'allegorical costumes'. In the late Victorian period, jewels set in star and crescent shapes were much in fashion, which no doubt influenced some of the dresses in this group. There were three representations of Night, an Astarte, Goddess of the Moon, and a Urania, Goddess of Astronomy, and in each case the outfits were lavishly embroidered with stars and moons, with diamond crescents and stars decorating the hair. Lady Gerard as Astarte was perhaps the most dramatically dressed of these. She wore a black accordion-pleated silk dress, with a short train studded with tiny gold stars and a belt made of diamond stars. On her head was a very striking diamond tiara in the shape of a half star with ten points, each at least six inches long.

———————— * ————————

Classical mythology provided many of the themes for costumes at the ball, and several of the most ingenious interpretations. RIGHT: *Lady Gerard as Astarte, Goddess of the Moon, looked both dramatic and pensive, with stars spangling her pleated dress, a star-shaped tiara, and an orb surmounted by a crescent moon.* ABOVE: *Lady Doreen Long took the theme of Urania, Goddess of Astronomy, embroidering her clothes with stars and moons*

Lady Terence Blackwood as Flora, covered her yellow
dress with wreathes and garlands of fresh flowers, and
wound lilies and orchids round her staff

Mrs Hope Vere adopted the serpentine look for
Medusa with squares of snakeskin on her dress and
snakes wound round her arms and body

Figures from classical mythology were much in evidence in this procession. Lady Terence Blackwood, as Flora, Goddess of Flowers, wore a stunning dress of pale yellow satin over an enormous crinoline, embroidered all over with wreaths and garlands of fresh flowers. On her head she wore a tiara with a wreath of flowers at the base, and she held a staff entwined with lilies and orchids and trailing leaves. In contrast to this, Mrs Hope Vere represented Medusa, with squares of snakeskin sewn to her dress, and snakes wound round her bodice and up her arms.

The last person to make her curtsey to the Prince and Princess of Wales was, suitably, Britannia, played by Lady Wolverton. Her costume was a dress of white crêpe de chine, the corsage forming a silver cuirasse with a sash over one shoulder bearing the Garter motto *'Honi soit qui mal y pense'*. She wore a helmet with white ostrich feather plumes, carried a shield and a three-pronged fork, and the long train stretched out behind her was a Union Jack.

After all the courts and groups had processed past the royal family, the single, dramatic figure of Lady Wolverton as Britannia made her appearance. Her shield and train were both based upon the Union Jack, while she wore over her shoulder a sash with the Garter motto, and on her head a helmet with the three white feathers of the Prince of Wales

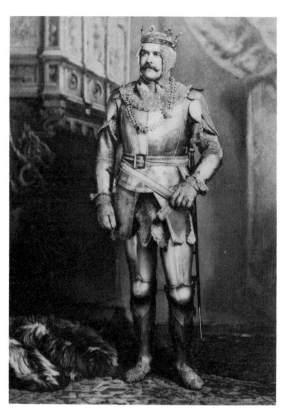

There was to have been a procession of the Court of Queen Guinevere and King Arthur's Knights of the Round Table, but because of the death of Marjorie Cavendish several of this court were unable to attend, and so it did not take place – much to the disappointment of Edith Chaplin, who described that in consequence she and her brother 'wandered around the ballroom like lost babes in the wood'. However, some of the knights and their ladies attended, and Lord and Lady Rodney agreed at the last moment to come as King Arthur and Queen Guinevere so that the splendid costumes should not go unused.

The men wore suits of armour that has been designed by Sir Edward Burne-Jones, of chain mail with plate armour over it. Each set was of a slightly different design, with poor King Arthur having the heaviest burden to carry, as his tunic and leggings were all of armour plate. Sir Galahad, played by the Hon. Grosvenor Hood, was more fortunate as he wore a silk tabard over his chain mail, with armour plating only on his arms. Sir John Lister Kaye went as Sir Kaye, from whom he claimed to be descended, and he had Sir Gareth, Sir Bedivere, Sir Perceval and Sir Tristram to keep him company. Queen Guinevere looked lovely in white crinkled silk crepe, and Lady Ashburton made a beautiful Enid in white velvet brocade. Mr Hall Walker must have deeply regretted not being able to make his impressive entrance as Merlin in a procession, as he looked so striking and convincing in silken robes embroidered with magic symbols, with locks of long white hair falling from beneath a rough turban.

———————— * ————————

The procession that never was: the Court of King Arthur.
The tragic death of little Marjorie Cavendish on the very day that the ball
took place meant that several members of the procession could not attend
at the last moment. Nevertheless Lord and Lady Rodney agreed to attend as
King Arthur and Queen Guinevere ABOVE : *with accompanying knights and ladies.*
BELOW LEFT :*Sir John Lister Kaye paid tribute to his putative ancestor,*
Sir Kaye Morte d'Arthur. BELOW RIGHT :*Mr and Mrs Hall*
Walker represented Merlin and Vivian

The processions enabled the guests both to exhibit their own outfits and to get a good view of what everyone else was wearing. They also gave a point to the costumes : putting them into some order made the occasion not only a ball, but a pageant of history as well, which contributed enormously to the success of the evening.

———————————— * ————————————

Family pride was very evident in some choices of costume. The Duke of Somerset (above) harked back to his illustrious ancestor, Edward Seymour, 1st Duke and Lord Protector of England in the reign of his nephew, Edward VI. His Duchess (right) portrayed the 1st Duke's sister, Jane Seymour, third Queen to Henry VIII and mother of Edward VI, in a costume clearly based upon Holbein's portrait

THE DUCHESS OF SOMERSET
*as Jane, Queen of England, wife of King Henry VIII
and mother to King Edward VI*

LADY MARGARET VILLIERS
as Lady Melbourne after Cosway

Lady Anne and Lady Dorothy Coventry, doubling up as Serena from a painting by George Romney. Whether this was the result of economy or to prevent sibling jealousy is not known

There were many lovely dresses worn by those not taking part in a procession, some of which had been copied from paintings of the wearers' ancestors. Countess Howe looked most impressive as the Lady Howe of 1796 after a painting by Gainsborough, and Lady Margaret Villiers made an elegant Caroline Lamb (Lady Melbourne) copied from a Cosway miniature. Lady Anne Coventry and her sister made the unusual choice of appearing in identical clothes, both representing Serena, from the painting by Romney. Maybe this was the sisters' own choice, maybe it was done for reasons of economy, or possibly their mother insisted upon it to prevent the sisters being jealous of each other's costumes.

--------------------- * ---------------------

Lady Margaret Villiers, daughter of the 5th Earl of Clarendon, copied her costume from Cosway's miniature of Caroline Lamb, lady Melbourne

Reuben Sassoon as a Persian Prince.
A close friend of the Prince of Wales,
'his shrewd touch with investments
was valued by a Patron whose Privy
Purse often wore thin'

Prince Victor Duleep Singh
representing the great Moghul
Emperor, Akbar

Some of the guests chose to represent characters from countries outside Europe. Reuben Sassoon looked most realistic as a Persian prince, and his daughter looked equally convincing as a Japanese lady in a beautiful silk-embroidered kimono. Prince Duleep Singh remained loyal to his country as the great Mogul Emperor, Akbar, while, nearer home, the Marquis of Tullibardine and Lord George Stewart-Murray appeared in national dress as eighteenth-century Highland gentlemen.

————————— * —————————

The Marquis of Tullibardine, heir to the Duke of Atholl, with his younger
brother, Lord George Stewart-Murray, as two Highland gentlemen at
the time of the '45 Rising

THE MARQUIS OF TULLIBARDINE
& LORD GEORGE STEWART-MURRAY
as two Highland gentlemen, 1745

Rival cardinals: Sir Henry Irving LEFT, *the great actor, played his role of
Cardinal Wolsey to perfection. The Earl of Dunraven* RIGHT *as Cardinal
Mazarin felt mortified by the comparison, 'for though I was a good presentment of
Mazarin in particular, Irving was certainly a better one of Cardinals in general'*

Everyone was much occupied with gazing at and congratulating each
other, though some were most annoyed to find after weeks of work and
preparation that they had a double even more convincing or well attired.
Lord Dunraven was one of these, and describing the occasion in his book,
Past Times and Pastimes, he recalled, 'I went as Cardinal Mazarin, and was
quite pleased with myself until late in the evening [Henry] Irving arrived
as another Cardinal. That was a beastly shame and quite put my nose out
of joint, for though I was a good presentment of Mazarin in particular,
Irving was certainly a better one of Cardinals in general.'

Lady Randolph Churchill in her memoirs described a similar incident. 'In one case a well known baronet had been perfecting himself for weeks in the role of Napoleon, his face and figure lending themselves to the impersonation. But what was his dismay at finding in the vestibule a second victor of Austerlitz even more life-like and correct than himself. It was indeed another Waterloo for both of them.'

After the processions had been completed and the guests had refreshed themselves with champagne, it was time for the quadrilles and dancing to begin. Each procession and court had its own quadrille, with the appropriate steps of the country or period that it represented, and, as *The Times* reported, 'nothing more harmonious could well be imagined than these slow dances walked through by magnificently dressed men, and by women whose beauty and jewelled costumes set off one another with all the charm of something strange, exceptional and unique'.

THE PROGRAMME OF DANCES

1. March	'Hungarian'	Berlioz
2. Overture	'Lustspiel'	Keler Béla
3. Valse	'Schatz'	Strauss
4. Csardas	'Huzzad Caigny'	Brahms
5. Morceau	'Minuet'	Paderewski
6. Czimbal Solo	'Rozca Volcsi'	Allaga
7. Valse	'Gartenlaube'	Strauss
8. Czimbal Solo	'Czak a Villagos'	Elemer
9. Valse	'Obersteiger'	Zeller
10. Morceau	'Souvenir de Moscow'	Proust
11. Csardas	'Korcsy Lany'	Sarkosy
12. Valse	'Verolbung'	Vullstedt
13. Czimbal Solo	'Ungarische Nepdal'	Krausse
14. Mazurka	'Mousmee'	Ganne
15. March		Sousa

Dancing was not undertaken with much enthusiasm except by the very young and energetic, for many of the guests were not suitably dressed for dancing, especially those in armour and those with long heavy trains. Lady Westmorland as Hebe with her stuffed eagle was not only unable to dance, but was considerably hampered when she tried to move around the crowded rooms. Others were too busy gazing at the scene around them or struggling to play up to their assumed parts.

On one occasion, the acting out of parts was carried a little too far. Jack Churchill, the seventeen-year-old son of Lady Randolph and younger brother of Winston, who represented a Louis XV courtier, got into a dispute with another young gentleman over a certain young lady. His mother described the incident:

Both losing their tempers they decided to settle the matter in the garden, and pulling out their weapons they began making some passes. But the combatants were unequally armed, one being a crusader with a double-handed sword, the other a Louis XV courtier armed with his rapier only. He, as might have been expected, got the worst of it, receiving a nasty cut on his pink silk stocking.

The Duke and Duchess were fortunate in having a warm clear night for the ball, and many guests strolled in the garden, which had been as elaborately decorated as the house. In the centre of the lawn was an eight-point star flanked by smaller stars at each corner, with the monogram D.D. and the snake crest of the Devonshires, the whole display being lit up with tiny lights. The oak and elm trees were outlined with Japanese lanterns, while the avenues to the east and west were festooned with Venetian lamps of blue and green, and the flower beds and gravel paths were picked out in red, white and blue fairy lights. In all, twelve thousand lamps shone in the garden, and with coloured fires that

———————————— * ————————————

The lovely gardens of Devonshire House stretched right back to Bolton Row and Lansdowne House, thus giving a park-like atmosphere in the middle of London. For the ball, twelve thousand lamps were bought in and must have made the gardens look like fairyland

burned at intervals, it was a scene of brilliant illumination. For those who wished to sit outside, a temporary verandah had been built round the house, roofed in with crimson and cream striped awnings under which were numerous chairs arranged amidst banks of flowers and ferns.

It was after midnight that the royal party, escorted by the Duke and Duchess, made their way to the supper room. This was a marquee reached by a staircase leading from one of the state rooms, but it was of such a substantial build, and so lavishly decorated inside, that few of the guests were even aware that they had left the house.

The floor was covered in thick crimson carpeting, and the walls were draped with blue and gold cloth upon which hung large mirrors and three Louis XIV tapestries depicting Roman scenes, lent to the Duke and Duchess by Messrs Duveen, the art dealers. Heavy crystal chandeliers hung from the ceiling, and at the far end of the marquee there was an enormous and splendid display of gold plate which had been sent down from Chatsworth.

There were twelve tables in the supper room, each one surrounding a palm after the fashion set by the Savoy Hotel the previous year. Hidden in the fronds of the palms, and in the flower arrangements around the marquee, were tiny electric lights which gave a glittering, fairy-like appearance to the room. The lights were an unusual novelty for those days, and by using them the Duchess was taking a risk. Electricity was still in its early days, and hostesses who chose this form of lighting were apt to find their ballrooms plunged into darkness without warning. Fortunately for the Duchess, however, all was well and the brilliant illuminations did not fail. As one newspaper pointed out, 'the electric light and the people themselves were the only modern things there, for not a guest, not a musician, not a herald, not a servant, nay, not even the ladies in the cloak-room were permitted to appear in a dress later than the beginning of the century'.

Supper was extremely difficult to organize, as the twelve tables each held only twelve guests at a time, and there were seven hundred to feed. The Duchess had arranged two sittings, with placement cards at each table making it quite clear who was to be at each sitting; after that the remaining guests could come in when they wished and seat themselves.

The menu was printed on a small white card five inches long by three and a half wide, surmounted by the ducal coronet and Devonshire House in gold.

SOUPER DU 2 JUILLET

Consommé Chaud et Froid
Poulet à la Diable
Côtelettes de Mouton aux Pois
Cailles Rôties

*   *   *

Crabe Rémoulade
Mousse de Saumon aux Concombres
Poulet en Mayonnaise
Noisette d'Agneau à l'Anglaise
Ortolans à l'Aspic
Sandwiches
Tomates à l'Algérienne
Salade à la Parmentière

*   *   *

Fraises à la Chantilly
Gelées; Pâtisserie
Macédoine de Fruits

Round the tables was a bizarre mixture of characters from every century and country, historical and fictional. At one table Dante's Beatrice sat beside Sir Thomas More, who in turn was next to Madame Recamier deep in conversation with her neighbour Sir Peter Teazle. On another Marie Antoinette and Lalla Rookh discussed the ball with King Arthur and Lord Darnley, while a servant dressed as an Egyptian slave handed round ortolans in aspic.

Inside the house the band played on, as the guests made their way to and from the supper room or sat and talked beneath the festoons of flowers and works of art that hung on the walls.

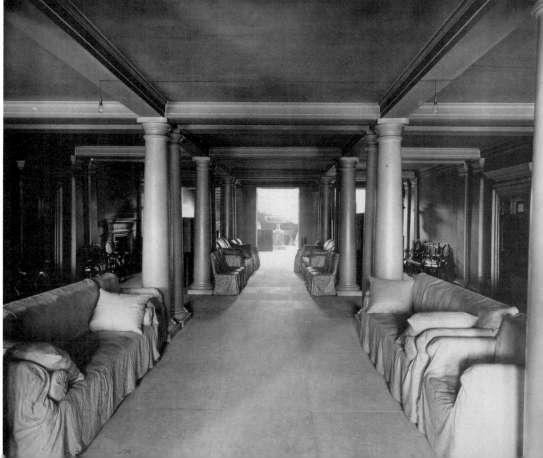

Politicians settled down for serious conversations on subjects that they had been debating in Parliament earlier in the week, although the political topics which they now discussed sounded somewhat incongruous coming from the mouths of a doge of Venice, a Louis XVI courtier and one of Cromwell's Roundheads.

Against the walls and on chairs lay various accessories which because of their inconvenience or discomfort had been discarded as the night wore on. Britannia's shield stood propped up beside Cleopatra's fan and Titiana's lily-entwined staff, while swords and visors and other pieces of armour were left on the floor by their hot and weary owners, and in some cases forgotten when the time came to go home.

Mothers and chaperones of debutantes talked with their friends, at the same time keeping an eye on their charges to make sure that there was no 'fast' behaviour taking place, such as dancing too frequently with the same man, or disappearing alone with a gentleman into the garden. The chaperones had an exhausting task, as they were obliged, however tired, to wait until their charges wished to go home.

Not until the early hours of the morning did the first guests make their farewells to the Duchess. As those leaving made their way back down the staircase, footmen were dispatched to alert the coachmen who, having spent the night talking and taking refreshment in the servants' hall, now hurried out to fetch their masters' carriages.

---------- * ----------

ABOVE: *The magnificent Ballroom at Devonshire House, scene of one of the most glittering social events of the century, being stripped ready for demolition.* BELOW: *The Little Hall at Devonshire House. Guests alighting at the front porch would pass through this hall to reach the marble staircase at the back of the house*

Most of the guests remained as long as possible in order to enjoy every moment of this unique occasion, and the sun was already rising when exhausted footmen and wan maids collected the guests' coats and called their carriages. All of them made their grateful thanks to the Duchess, congratulating her with every superlative they knew on her wonderful ball. Downstairs, as the sun brightened over Green Park, they waited, still talking excitedly, for their carriages to be announced.

Outside, the crowd that had gathered to watch the arrivals had dispersed, and except for a few carts making early morning deliveries, it was through a silent and deserted Mayfair that the smart broughams made their homeward journeys.

The Duchess of Marlborough in her autobiography wrote a sad recollection of her walk home across the park:

The Ball lasted to the early hours of the morning, and the sun was rising as I walked through Green Park to Spencer House where we then lived. On the grass were the dregs of humanity. Human beings too dispirited or sunk to find work or favour, they sprawled in sodden stupor, pitiful representatives of the submerged tenth. In my billowing period dress I must have seemed to them a vision of wealth and youth, and I thought soberly that they must hate me. But they only looked, and some even had a compliment to enliven my progress.

Already the shadow of change was approaching.

For Lady Randolph Churchill, and her sister Leonie Leslie, however, the excitements of the night were not yet over. On their way to their houses near Marble Arch, they met a travelling circus from which a camel put its head into their brougham, and, according to Mrs Leslie, was amazed by the strangely dressed occupants.

Elsewhere in Mayfair and Belgravia weary guests were arriving home, to sleep, and then to wake as *The Times'* reporter lyrically put it, 'upon a world that must indeed seem commonplace in comparison with the jewelled page of romance upon which for a moment they gazed last night'.

$\mathcal{A}$LL the daily newspapers and weekly magazines in Britain gave the ball full coverage, with headlines such as 'The Duchess's Great Ball', 'Revelry at Devonshire House', 'Crowds of Mimic Kings and Queens', and 'Extraordinary Social Function'. Even papers from places as far distant as New York reported it, and some of their accounts, although lavish, were written with more drama than accuracy.

The day after the ball the house was reorganized and the furniture replaced in the reception rooms, but the entertainments were still not over for the Duke and Duchess and their household. On the following Tuesday there was a garden party at Devonshire House given mainly for the foreign dignitaries and colonial Prime Ministers in England for the Jubilee, whom the Duchess had had neither the room nor inclination to invite to the ball, but for whom some sort of reception was deemed necessary.

For all those who had attended the ball, the rest of the season's entertainments must have seemed very flat. As the preparations beforehand had been the chief topic of conversation in society, so was discussing the ball itself the main subject for many months afterwards, much to the chagrin, no doubt, of those who had not been invited.

The beautiful costumes were put away, in many cases never to be worn again. Some are still in existence, including that of the Duchess which is in remarkably good condition. Others were cut up, the fine old embroideries and lace being used as additions to other frocks, while some no doubt eventually found their way into family dressing-up boxes.

After the ball, life as society had known it was to continue for another seventeen years, though becoming ever more precarious as social change accelerated.

Queen Victoria died, greatly mourned, in 1901, and her death marked in several senses the end of an era. Without the great imperial figurehead, confidence in the Empire, already damaged by the Boer War, flagged still further. Britain was no longer 'the workshop of the world', having been overtaken in many industrial fields by Germany, the United States and Japan. But it was the increasing shift to the left, demonstrated in the rout of the Conservatives by the Liberals in the 1906 General Election, that most affected the way of life of the ruling class. The social reform that followed, and the consequent rise in public spending, had to be paid for in increased taxes: super tax, the taxing of unearned income, and higher death duties dealt mortal blows to the aristocracy.

Concerned as they were at the continuing threat to their security, they still carried on during the early years of the twentieth century with their frenetic round of social activities and entertainments, and maintained their big houses on as lavish a scale as ever. With the advances in transport country house weekends had become popular, and in many households gleaming motor cars were replacing the landaus and Victorias.

The death of Edward VII in 1910 brought about further change in society. His successor, George V, (the Duke of York at the Devonshire House Ball) was a more serious-minded monarch, who cared much less for grand entertainments than had his pleasure-loving father, and many a hostess must have mourned the passing of the sparkle and glamour of life in the Marlborough House set.

All too soon, life as society had known it for so long was to come to an abrupt end. In 1914 the Great War broke out, and within four years a whole generation of young men had been wiped out, and the social structure of Britain had changed completely. For those who twenty-one years before had been gaily preparing for the Devonshire House Ball, the world would never be the same again.

The Duke and Duchess did not live to witness this great upheaval. Harty Tarty had died in 1908, greatly mourned by his friends and political contemporaries, and most of all by his wife. She followed him three years later, when, powerful and energetic to the end, she suffered a fatal stroke whilst attending Sandown Races.

Devonshire House, too, was a tragic victim of the social change. The 9th Duke and his Duchess, in common with many of their friends, considered that the days of big London houses were over, and that their lovely home in the heart of London was a superfluous and unnecessary expense. Property redevelopment was taking place on a large scale all over London, and it never occurred to anyone then that these beautiful and historic houses should be preserved. In 1919 the Devonshire family sold Devonshire House, well knowing what its fate would be, to property developers for one million pounds, and in 1924, in an act of wanton destruction, it was demolished. On its site, and in what was once the lovely garden, are now hideous blocks of flats and offices.

The end of Devonshire House: William Kent's one London private palace being reduced to rubble in 1924. The lovely gardens have already been turned into a building site

[169]

All that remains are the wrought-iron entrance gates which stand between Green Park and Piccadilly, a sad reminder of the beautiful house and the glittering ball held within its walls.

SELECTED READING

Asquith, Henry, *Memories and Reflections*, 1928

Asquith, Margot, *Off the Record*, 1943
Autobiography, 1920

Balsan, Consuelo, *The Glitter and the Gold*, New York, 1952

Baring, Maurice, *The Puppet Show of Memory*, 1922

Benson, E.F., *As We Were*, 1930

Beresford, Lord William, *Memoirs*, 1914

Blyth, Henry, *Skittles*, 1970
The Pocket Venus, 1966

Camplin, Jamie, *The Rise of the Plutocrats*, 1978

Chancellor, E.B., *Private Palaces of London*, 1908

Churchill, Lady Randolph, *Reminiscences*, 1908

Crewe, The Marquess of, *Lord Rosebery*, 1931

Dunraven, Lord, *Past Times and Pastimes*, 1922

Eliot, Elizabeth, *They all Married Well*, 1959

Esher, Lord, *Cloud Capped Towers*, 1927
Extracts from Journals 1872-1895

Fane, Lady Augusta, *Chit Chat*, 1926

Fingall, Lady, *Seventy Years Young*, 1937

Forbes, Lady Angela, *Memories and Base Details*, 1922

Holland, Bernard, *Life of the Duke of Devonshire*, 1911

Leslie, Anita, *Edwardians in Love*, 1972
The Fabulous Leonard Jerome, 1954
Jennie, 1969

Leveson-Gower, Lord Ronald, *Records and Reminscences*, 1883

Londonderry, The Marchioness of, *Retrospect*, 1938

Menzies, Mrs Stuart, *Lord William Beresford*, 1917

Morris, James, *Pax Britannica*, 1968

Portland, Duke of, *Men, Women and Things*, 1937

Radziwill, Princess Catherine, *My Recollections*, 1904

Ralph, James, *Critical Review of the Publick (sic) Buildings etc. in London*, 1734

Ribblesdale, Lady Emma, *Letters and Diaries*, 1930

Shepherd, Gordon Brook, *Uncle of Europe*, 1975

Sutherland, Douglas, *The Yellow Earl*, 1963

Turner, E.S., *The Court of St James's*, 1960

Warwick, Lady, *Afterthoughts*, 1931
Memories of Sixty Years, 1917

West, George Cornwallis, *Edwardian Heydays*, 1930

Williams, Mrs Hwfa, *It was Such Fun*, 1935

Worth, J.P., *A Century of Fashion*, 1928

INDEX

LIST OF COSTUMES

Akbar, Emperor of India
  Prince Victor Duleep Singh
Almada, Count
  Marquis de Soveral
Andrillon, Princesse
  Countess of Minto
Anne of Austria, Empress
  Duchess of Manchester
D'Artagnan
  William James
Arthur, King
  Lord Rodney
Astarte
  Lady Gerard
Bacelli, Signora
  Lady Beatrice Herbert
Beatrice
  Countess of Mar and Kellie
Berenice, Queen of Palestine
  Countess of Essex
Bess of Hardwick
  Duchess of Roxburghe
Bingham, Lady Anne
  Lady Eva Dugdale
Britannia
  Lady Wolverton
Catherine the Great, Empress
of Russia
  Viscountess Raincliffe
Charles V, Holy Roman
Emperor
  Duke of Devonshire
Cleopatra (2)
  *Countess de Grey, Mrs Arthur
  Paget*
Coldstream Guard
  Marquis of Winchester
Coligny, Admiral
  Earl de Grey
Corday, Charlotte
  Duchess of Sutherland

Cornaro, Caterina
  *Mrs Hwfa Williams (did not
  attend)*
Cranmer, Archbishop
Thomas
  Lord Rowton
Cumberland, Earl of
  George, Duke of York
Cydalise
  Emily Yznaga
Cyprus, King of
  Ivor Wimborne
Darnley Henry Stewart, Lord
  John Leslie
Edward the Black Prince
  Colonel Arthur Paget
Eighteenth century,
gentleman of
  Earl of Rosebery
Elaine the Lily Maid of Astolat
  Edith Chaplin
Elizabeth I, Queen
  Baroness Tweedmouth
Enid
  Lady Ashburton
Essex, Countess of
  Countess of Lonsdale
Essex, Robert Devereux,
Earl of
  Earl of Essex
Esther, Queen of Israel
  Countess of Dudley
Euterpe
  Mrs Ronalds
Flora
  Lady Terence Blackwood
France, gentleman of
  Reginald Brett
Francis of Lorraine, Consort
Emperor of Austria
  Viscount Castlereagh

Frederick Henry,
Duke/Prince of Nassau
  Alfred Beit
French Ambassador to Russia
and wife
  *Duke and Duchess of
  Marlborough*
French Court of King Henry
II, gentleman and lady of
  Duke and Duchess of Fife
French Court of King Henry
IV, ladies of
  *Princess Maud,
  Princess Victoria,
  Duchess of York*
Furies
  *Lady Lurgan,
  Lady Sophie Scott*
Galahad, Sir
  Hon. Grosvenor Hood
Genoa, lady of
  Lady Helen Vincent
Guinevere, Queen
  *Marchioness of Ormonde (did
  not attend, replaced by Lady
  Rodney)*
Guise, Duchess de
  Lady Lister Kaye
Harcourt, Simon, Lord
  Sir William Harcourt
Hebe
  Sibyl, Countess of Westmorland
Henry III, King of France
  Count Albert Mensdorff
Highland gentlemen
  *Marquis of Tullibardine,
  Lord George Stewart-Murray*
Holland, gentleman of
  Arthur Balfour
Italian courtier
  Earl of Dudley

Jane Seymour, Queen
  Duchess of Somerset
Johannes Palaeologus, Holy
Roman Emperor
  George Wyndham
Kaunitz, Prince
  Marquis of Lansdowne
Kaye Morte d'Arthur, Sir
  Sir John Lister Kaye
Keith, Lady
  Marchioness of Lansdowne
Lamballe, Princesse de
  Lady Algernon Gordon Lennox
Laura
  Lady Stavordale
Lefebvre, Marshal
  Rt. Hon. Henry Chaplin
Leicester, Robert Dudley,
Earl of
  Baron Tweedmouth
Lowther, Sir Richard
  Earl of Lonsdale
Maria Theresa, Empress of
Austria
  Marchioness of Londonderry
Marie Antoinette, Queen of
France
  Countess of Warwick
Marie de'Medici, Queen of
France
  Mrs William Grenfell
Mary, Queen of Scots
  Lady Edmonstone
Mazarin, Cardinal
  Lord Dunraven
Medusa
  Mrs Hope Vere
Melbourne, Lady
  Lady Edith Villiers
Mercutio
  William Grenfell

[175]

Merlin
Mr Hall Walker
Nevers, Duchess de
Countess of Alington
Orloff, Prince
Prince of Pless
Persian prince
Reuben Sassoon
Petrarch
Lord Stavordale
Polignac, Madame de
Mrs George Keppel
Poniatowski, Prince
Lord Henry Bentinck
Romeo
Lord Hyde
Roundhead soldier
Herbert Asquith

Rutland, Mary Isabella,
Duchess of
Marchioness of Granby
de Sada, Laura
Lady Alice Montagu
St John of Jerusalem, Grand
Prior of the Order of
Prince of Wales
Sauvio, Duca and Duchessa di
Duke and Duchess of Portland
Scheherazade
May Goelet
Serena (2)
*Lady Anne and Lady Dorothy
Coventry*
Sheba, Queen of (2)
*Princess of Pless,
Dowager Countess of Dudley*

Snake charmer
Margot Asquith
Somers, Will
Henry Holden
Somerset, Edward Seymour,
Duke of
Duke of Somerset
Sophia of Hanover, Electress
Mary, Duchess of Teck
Theodora, Empress of
Byzantium
Lady Randolph Churchill
Urania
Lady Doreen Long
Valkyrie
Hon. Mrs Reginald Talbot
Valois, Queen Marguerite de
Princess of Wales

Vashti
Muriel Wilson
Velazquez
Sir Ernest Cassel
Venice, Doges of
Earl of Lathom, Viscount Pee
Venice, page to Dogaressa o
Evelyn de Rothschild
Visconti, Valentina (2)
Lady Robert Cecil
Hon. Mrs George Curzon
Vivian
Mrs Hall Walker
Wolsey, Cardinal
Sir Henry Irving
Zenobia, Queen of Palmyra
Duchess of Devonshire

[176]